TRANSPORTATION ISSUES, POLICIES AND R&D

MITIGATING SUICIDES ON RAILWAYS

COUNTERMEASURES AND LESSONS

TRANSPORTATION ISSUES, POLICIES AND R&D

Additional books in this series can be found on Nova's website under the Series tab.

Additional e-books in this series can be found on Nova's website under the e-book tab.

TRANSPORTATION ISSUES, POLICIES AND R&D

MITIGATING SUICIDES ON RAILWAYS

COUNTERMEASURES AND LESSONS

FRANCES DIAZ
EDITOR

nova publishers
New York

Library of Congress Cataloging-in-Publication Data

ISBN: 978-1-63484-135-1

Published by Nova Science Publishers, Inc. † New York

CONTENTS

Preface

Trespassing is the leading cause of rail-related fatalities in the United States. A large proportion of these trespasser fatalities are from intentional acts (i.e., suicides). With a lack of systematic research and evaluation of the countermeasures that are currently in place as well as those that have been proposed, it is difficult for railroad carriers and communities that seek to select appropriate countermeasures that are likely to be effective at mitigating suicides. This book discusses the current information available on trespasser fatalities and the implementation of countermeasures in use internationally to prevent suicides on the railroad right-of-way. The book presents a discussion of each countermeasure according to various intervention points along the path to complete suicide on the railroad right-of-way.

In: Mitigating Suicides on Railways
Editor: Frances Diaz
ISBN: 978-1-63484-135-1

Chapter 1

COUNTERMEASURES TO MITIGATE INTENTIONAL DEATHS ON RAILROAD RIGHTS-OF-WAY: LESSONS LEARNED AND NEXT STEPS*

Scott H. Gabree, Stephanie Chase, Ann Doucette and Michael Martino

ABSTRACT

Trespassing is the leading cause of rail-related fatalities in the United States. A large proportion of these trespasser fatalities are from intentional acts (i.e., suicides). With a lack of systematic research and evaluation of the countermeasures that are currently in place as well as those that have been proposed, it is difficult for railroad carriers and communities that seek to select appropriate countermeasures that are likely to be effective at mitigating suicides. This report discusses the current information available on trespasser fatalities and the implementation of countermeasures in use internationally to prevent suicides on the railroad right-of-way. The paper presents a discussion of each countermeasure according to various intervention points along the path to complete suicide on the railroad right-of-way. These intervention

* This is an edited, reformatted and augmented version of a Technical Report, DOT/FRA/ORD-14/36, sponsored by the U.S. Department of Transportation, Federal Railroad Administration and issued November 2014.

points include: preventing individuals from reaching a suicidal state, making the railroad environment appear to be a less viable means for attempting suicide, deterring access to the right-of-way, avoiding collisions with trespassers and pedestrians, reducing the lethality of a train-person collision, and improving the quality of data and reporting standards. Each of these intervention points provides an opportunity for a countermeasure to potentially divert the individual from the path towards a suicidal act.

EXECUTIVE SUMMARY

In 2010, 38,364 individuals intentionally ended their lives in the United States[1]. It is estimated that less than 1 percent of those individuals took their lives on railroad rights-of-way. Despite the relatively small percentage of suicides on the rights-of-way, these incidents greatly impact not only the individuals involved and their family and friends, but also train crews, first responders, and bystanders. The railroad carriers are also impacted by the resulting operational disruptions and delays and the need to address the potentially debilitating physical and psychological effects on those involved in the incident.

Though percentage of all suicides in the United States, suicides on railroad rights-of-way represent a significant number of all railroad fatalities. In 2012, 242 fatalities were determined by a coroner or medical examiner to be suicides. During that same time period, the railroad industry experienced 429 trespasser fatalities (non-suicide) and 232 grade crossing fatalities, indicating that suicides were the second leading cause of death on the railroad rights-of-way. As passenger and freight railroad traffic increases, these rates are likely to climb.

This report examines suicide countermeasure strategies which have been specifically implemented or conceived for implementation in the railroad environment. These countermeasure strategies are organized into sections based on how or when the strategy proposes to mitigate suicide actions. The sections included are:

- 3.1 Reduction or Prevention of Suicidal Ideation in the Railroad Environment
- 3.2 Reduction of Perceived Viability of Railroad Right-of-Way as Means for Suicide
- 3.3 Prevention of Access to Tracks

3.4 Increased Ability to Avoid a Train-Person Collision
3.5 Reduction in Lethality of Train-Person Collision
3.6 Improvement in Data Collection

Each countermeasure discussed includes the following information: current use; evidence of effectiveness for rail; evidence of effectiveness for other means; evidence of impacts on other individuals; and, finally, feasibility of implementation in the railroad environment.

No single countermeasure is likely to fit every railroad carrier or every situation. Therefore, this document is intended to serve simply as a reference that helps railroad carriers better understand what evidence exists for, or against, the likelihood of each countermeasure effectively reducing suicides on their rights-of-way. In many cases, a combination of countermeasures may be most effective.

1. Introduction

In 2010, 38,364 individuals intentionally ended their lives in the United States[2]. It is estimated that less than 1 percent of those individuals took their lives on railroad rights-of-way. Despite a small percentage of suicides occurring on rights-of-way, these incidents greatly impact not only the individuals involved and their family and friends, but also train crews, first responders, bystanders, and society at large. The railroad carriers are also impacted by the resulting service disruptions, delays, and the need to address the potentially debilitating physical and psychological effects on those involved in the incident.

In the United States, determining the exact number of suicides that occur on the railroad rights- of-way is difficult. Additionally, state medical privacy laws may preclude the release of certain types of data. Prior to June 2011, the Federal Railroad Administration (FRA) did not systematically collect any information about suicide incidents because FRA Accident/Incident reporting explicitly excluded fatalities on the railroad right-of-way officially determined to be a suicide by a medical examiner or coroner.[3] As a result of the Rail Safety Improvement Act of 2008 (RSIA), FRA removed this exemption in June 2011 and began to collect incident reports of suicide as specified by the revised Code of Federal Regulations (CFR) and reflected in the FRA Guide for Preparing Accident/Incident Reports[4]. 49 CFR Part 225.41 was updated and now reads, “FRA does not include suicide data (as defined in §225.5) in its periodic summaries of data on the number of injuries and illnesses associated with railroad operations. FRA will maintain suicide data in a database that is not publicly accessible. Suicide data will not be available on FRA's Web site for individual reports or downloads. Suicide data will be available to the public in aggregate format on FRA's website and via requests under the Freedom of Information Act." Suicide data reported to FRA by railroads was released by FRA in an aggregate form for the first time in late 2013. Prior to this change in the FRA regulations, estimates of the prevalence of suicides on the railroad rights-of-way in the United States could only be obtained directly from cooperating railroads or through media reporting. Current FRA data show that in 2012 there were 242 suicide fatalities and 46 additional injuries from suicide attempts. As of the publication of this report, 2012 was the only year with suicide data available through FRA—collection of this information is ongoing so all data from July 2012 onward will eventually be reported.

To better understand the characteristics of individuals who die on the railroad rights-of-way in the United States, the Cadle Creek Consulting group (under contract to FRA's Office of Railroad Safety) analyzed the FRA trespass fatality reports from 2002 to 2004 on the FRA Office of Safety Analysis Web site with the ultimate goal of developing trespassing prevention outreach or public education strategies. Since researchers could not rely on incident reports to use the words "intentional" or "suicide" to describe a fatal incident, they subjectively attempted to determine if a given incident was a probable suicide based on the report's narrative description of the incident. This research effort found that 18 percent of FRA trespass fatality reports (167 out of 935 reported fatalities) submitted to FRA by railroads included the word "suicide" or "intentional" to describe the fatal incident. An additional 5 percent (49 incidents) without the inclusion of "intentional" or "suicide" were subjectively determined to be a "probable suicide." Findings show that approximately 18–23 percent of FRA reported trespasser fatalities between 2002 and 2004 could be classified as suicides or probable suicides. This range likely underestimates the total number of suicides that took place on railroad rights-of-way because any incidents determined to be a suicide by a coroner or medical examiner were not reported by railroads, or likely had already been removed from the FRA database, as noted above.

Researchers have estimated the prevalence of suicide on railroad rights-of-way using a number of different data sources, including State mortality surveillance systems, railroad trespasser fatality records, and media reports (Martino, Gabree, and Chase, 2013). Using these sources, the researchers found that between June 1, 2006, and May 31, 2007 (12 months), 268 fatalities on the railroad right-of-way were identified as suicides, while FRA had reported a total of 497 trespasser fatalities. It is not known how many of the 268 confirmed suicides were included in FRA's 497 trespasser fatalities; however, reporting guidelines during this timeframe directed railroads to remove all suicides, which indicates that a minimum of 35 percent of all trespasser fatalities during this timeframe were deemed to be the result of a suicide.[5] Similarly, between July 1, 2007, and May 31, 2010, (36 months), 428 fatalities were determined to be suicides, while FRA reported 1,341 trespasser fatalities during this timeframe, indicating that a minimum of 24 percent of all trespasser fatalities during the timeframe were the result of a suicide. Based on various factors, including inconsistent reporting by railroads during this second phase of the study, this estimate is believed to be an underrepresentation of the actual number of suicides committed during this time frame.[6]

The majority of suicides which occur on the railroad rights-of-way are the result of an individual trespassing.[7] Trespassers are defined as "persons who are on the part of railroad property used in railroad operation and whose presence is prohibited, forbidden, or unlawful."[8] Though suicides typically fall into this category, suicides are treated differently from trespasser fatalities and are stored in a separate database. After suicide events are separated, trespasser fatalities alone are still the leading cause of rail-related deaths in the United States. When suicide countermeasures are designed, it is important to consider impacts on both suicide and trespass fatalities, as the two are often the result of a similar physical action, albeit with different intentions. Of the 937 total fatalities reported in 2012, 543 were trespass incidents and 242 were classified as suicide incidents, indicating that 84 percent of all fatalities were either trespass or suicide-related.[9]

Already a concern for the railroad industry, the number of trespassing incidents is likely to grow as the use of public transportation increases across the nation. In 2009, 10.4 billion trips were taken by passengers on public transportation of all kinds (bus, rail, van pool, etc.) in the United States, and the use of trains for public transportation continues to grow.[10] In FY 2013, 31.6 million passengers rode on Amtrak; this was the largest recorded ridership in Amtrak history and the tenth ridership record in the past 11 years.[11] With this increase in ridership comes an increase in opportunities for incidents, such as trespasser or grade crossing collisions, and thus an increased need to ensure that those who ride the railroad system are safe and delays in commutes are minimized. As a part of an effort to accomplish this goal, FRA allocates funding every year to attempt to reduce the number of trespasser fatalities. Though trespasser prevention is emphasized, suicides on the railroad right-of-way may be overlooked when trespasser-specific research and countermeasures, actions taken, or strategies implemented to reduce or prevent undesired outcomes are developed. Suicide and trespasser fatalities have nearly identical impact on the railroad industry in terms of cost or delays. The difference between the two is in the intent or motivation of the individual involved; a trespasser willfully ignores legal prohibitions on entering private property and then either misjudges or is unaware of an oncoming train, whereas an individual attempting suicide is intent on being struck and killed by a train. Obviously, countermeasures for one group may not be generalizable to the other and may in fact have different effects. The countermeasures need to be designed and evaluated in terms of their effectiveness for both groups—those intent on suicide and those who trespass on the railroad property.

Researchers have investigated countermeasures to mitigate suicide in a general sense (i.e., not railway specific suicides, but suicides by all means). Much of this research has focused on identifying individuals who may be exhibiting risk factors or warning signs for suicide. For example, over 90 percent of individuals who die by suicide have been diagnosed with a mental health disorder (National Alliance of Mental Health – NAMI suicide fact sheet, accessed March 2014). Substance abuse (drug or alcohol) has also been noted as a risk factor (Goldston, 2004). If researchers are able to identify the population with the highest risk for suicide, they can ensure that individuals seen exhibiting these attributes are referred to a mental health professional. However, assessing treatment options for individuals with suicidal ideation from a clinical point of view is not applicable to railroads and thus is not in the purview of this document. Instead, this document aims to assess what strategies might be implemented in the railroad environment to mitigate suicides on the rights-of-way.

1.1. Objectives

The purpose of this report is to provide an overview of suicide mitigation efforts (countermeasures) that have already been implemented or have been conceived for implementation in the United States or worldwide. The goal of this document is to provide a comprehensive list of countermeasures, each one documenting critical research and evidence describing the countermeasure in order to inform those who may be in the process of developing countermeasures.

1.2. Organization of the Report

This document lists countermeasures to mitigate suicides on railroad rights-of-way. The various strategies listed have been implemented or conceived for implementation in the railroad environment. Section 2 briefly discusses the role of the railroad industry in the mitigation of suicides on railroad rights-of-way before examining individual countermeasure strategies in Section 3. Countermeasure strategies are organized into sections based on how or when they mitigate suicide actions. The sections included are:

- 3.1 Reduction or Prevention of Suicidal Ideation in the Railroad Environment
- 3.2 Reduction of Perceived Viability of Railroad Right-of-Way as Means for Suicide
- 3.3 Prevention of Access to the Right-of-Way
- 3.4 Increased Ability to Avoid a Train-Person Collision
- 3.5 Reduction in Lethality of Train-Person Collision
- 3.6 Improvement in Data Collection

2. Role for Railroad Carriers

The railroad industry is ostensibly concerned about individuals who use the track as a means to attempt suicide and those who may witness or assist in the management of the potentially post- traumatic event. Although the railroad is not able to identify suicidal individuals, or directly assist them in seeking treatment, railroad carriers may be in a position to attempt to block the means of suicide at certain locations or provide resources (such as crisis hot line number on signage) to deter individuals from attempting or dying as a result of the act on railroad right-of- way. Such mitigation strategies may be implemented by the railroad carrier or in cooperation with local communities or care providers. There is no "correct" way to mitigate or prevent suicide on the railroad rights-of-way. Such events are but one of the dynamic environmental risks and factors that must be taken into consideration on a daily basis. Thus, each railroad typically assesses its particular concerns in terms of when and how these incidents are occurring, their relative impact and any legal duty or standard of care, and then plan a course of action which is most likely to be effective.

For example, railroad stations are highly visible and accessible locations through which large numbers of individuals pass. Mitigation strategies could involve disseminating information about available help services and training personnel to observe, monitor, and report behaviors that may indicate high risk individuals at or around the station. This strategy would, however, have numerous liability implications and consequences, and be of no use to freight operations, which do not frequent passenger stations. Many rail-related suicides occur on the open track with little to no monitoring. Although ideally the railroad carrier restricts access to the entire right-of-way, that is likely not feasible either physically or financially (see Section 3.3.2 – Means Restriction for additional information). However, the railroads may be able to identify and develop ways to physically restrict access to locations of concern on their rights-of-way to reduce the possibility of such incidents occurring, especially at "hotspot" locations.[12]

The remainder of this document will discuss countermeasures proposed to mitigate suicides on the railroad right-of-way. Each countermeasure discussed includes at least some railroad carrier participation. While not all countermeasures presented are recommended or even feasible for railroads to adopt, they may provide insight into effective mitigation strategies for the railroad right-of-way.

3. Proposed Rail-Specific Countermeasures

Reducing an individual's suicidal ideation is the initial step of any suicide countermeasure effort. Though reducing suicidal ideation through clinical means is beyond the purview of the railroad, there are some strategies that can be employed to reduce the likelihood that an individual will attempt suicide. The purpose of Figure 1 is to illustrate the process which an individual may take in considering suicide on the railroad right-of-way as well as where countermeasures might be most effectively implemented. The shaded boxes along the left side of the diagram illustrate the suicidal process and the boxes to the right indicate opportunity for intervention. The goal of suicide countermeasures is to interrupt the flow of this diagram at some point, at least temporarily and, ideally, permanently. Successful countermeasures will prevent an individual from progressing down the diagram.

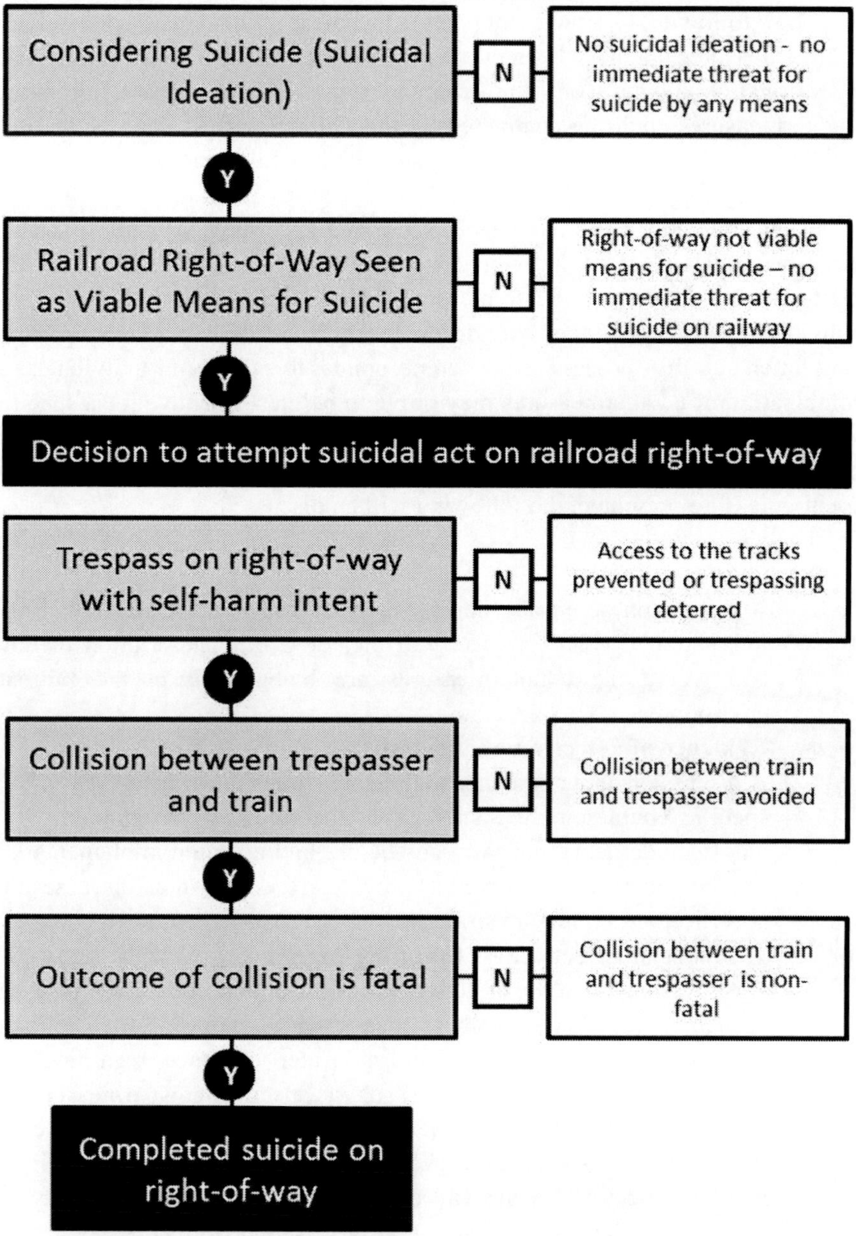

Figure 1. Process Leading to Death by Suicide on Right-of-Way.

The following sections of this document will focus on suicide countermeasures that have been proposed or implemented with a specific goal: to mitigate suicides on the railroad right-of-way. These proposed countermeasures could be completed by the railroad, either alone or through collaboration between another partner such as a local community or suicide prevention group.

Each countermeasure has been categorized according to where it would theoretically interrupt an individual's path toward a suicide attempt on the right-of-way. A single countermeasure is unlikely to deter or stop all individuals from attempting suicide on the railroad. Since countermeasures may interrupt this process at different points for different individuals, a combination of countermeasures may prove to be most effective for a specific railroad or physical location. Multiple countermeasures may act as safeguards if preceding countermeasure(s) are unsuccessful. For each possible countermeasure presented, the following will be discussed:

- **Current Use**
  A discussion about any current or past uses in the United States or internationally. This section will include a brief description of how and where the countermeasures are being used in the railroad environment.
- **Evidence of Effectiveness for Rail**
  A discussion about evidence that demonstrates the effectiveness of the specific countermeasure strategy in the railroad environment. This may include data from railroads before and after the implementation of a countermeasure, as well as previous research which discusses the specific countermeasure strategy.
- **Evidence of Effectiveness for Other Means**
  A discussion about the effectiveness of the countermeasure strategy in reducing suicide by other means (i.e., not in the railroad environment). This section will consider evidence regarding the effectiveness (or lack thereof) of a specific countermeasure in reducing suicides by other means. There is no guarantee, however, that countermeasures to prevent suicide by other means will be equally effective in the railroad environment. The Feasibility of Railroad Implementation section discusses this issue.
- **Evidence of Impact on Other Individuals**
  A discussion of evidence on the potential impacts of each countermeasure on other individuals, such as trespassers (without

suicidal intent) and railroad passengers who may not be the intended prevention audience. This section will consider any evidence available regarding the impact of a specific countermeasure on non-suicidal individuals.

- **Feasibility of Railroad Implementation**
  A discussion of feasibility for the railroad to implement the countermeasure. This section will describe the potential cost of implementation, as well as the likelihood of/evidence for effectiveness in the railroad environment. Due to differences in freight and passenger railroad operations, feasibility for each operation will be discussed separately.

It is important to keep in mind that the *Proposed Rail-Specific Countermeasures* section of this report includes countermeasures that have been proposed regardless of the implementation feasibility for the railroad, regulators, other organizations, nor with respect to existing Federal, State and local laws, ordinances, or case law. Therefore, not every countermeasure is recommended for adoption, or even consideration. No one means of prevention is necessarily better or worse than any other or most likely to have the greatest impact; each will depend on the situation, railroad, and community. Additionally, while many countermeasures exist to reduce the likelihood of suicides by other means (e.g., mental health interventions not focused on the railway), the focus of this document is restricted to the railroad environment.

3.1. Reduction or Prevention of Suicidal Ideation in the Railroad Environment

Reducing the overall number of individuals who attempt suicide by all means will likely result in a decrease in suicides on the railroad rights-of-way. However, suicides on the rights-of-way account for less than 1 percent of all suicides in the United States; the majority of suicides in the United States involve firearms, suffocation, or poisoning.[13] Many organizations around the world, including the World Health Organization (WHO)[14], the International Association for Suicide Prevention (IASP), and the U.S. Department of Health and Human Services (HHS), are currently working to address concerns about suicide by all means.[15] While the role of the railroad in suicide prevention focuses primarily on preventing suicides on the railroad rights-of-way, some of its suicide mitigation countermeasures may in fact deter suicide by other means. The schematic in Figure 2 shows the potential impact of countermeasures which aim to reduce or prevent an individual's suicidal ideation. A red "X" over the circle with a "Y" (i.e., a "Yes") indicates that this path has been blocked, at least temporarily. While reducing or preventing suicidal ideation through a countermeasure may not prevent an individual from ever attempting suicide, it may delay those thoughts or prompt an individual to seek the help he or she needs. Each grayed-out box represents a potential action or belief that is mitigated if a countermeasure is effective.

The following section discusses potential countermeasures that could be used in a railroad environment to reduce an individual's suicidal ideation. These countermeasures may impact not only individuals who consider completing suicide on the railroad rights-of-way, but also those who use the railway system and may have considered suicide by another means. Countermeasures included in this section are all discussed in terms of how the railroad industry may be able to help reduce suicidal ideation, a task which is often considered outside the scope of the railroad's responsibility. The countermeasures discussed in this section include:

- Blue Lights – Installation of blue lights in railway stations has been initiated to reduce suicide rates through the properties of the light itself. This installation has been seen at railroad stations in Japan.
- Gatekeeper Training – The training of station personnel or other authorized individuals to identify at-risk behaviors and intervene appropriately.
- Public Awareness Campaigns (Suicide Focused) – An effort to educate the general public about suicide on the railroad rights-of-way via advertisements and targeted messaging.
- Signage (Crisis Center) – Placing signage that promotes crisis hotlines, intervention services, or sources of counseling in railroad stations and near the open tracks in order to encourage individuals with suicidal intent to call the hotline number before deciding to take their lives.
- Training of Mental Health Providers – Supplying mental healthcare providers with sufficient information to heighten awareness about suicides on railroad rights-of-way.

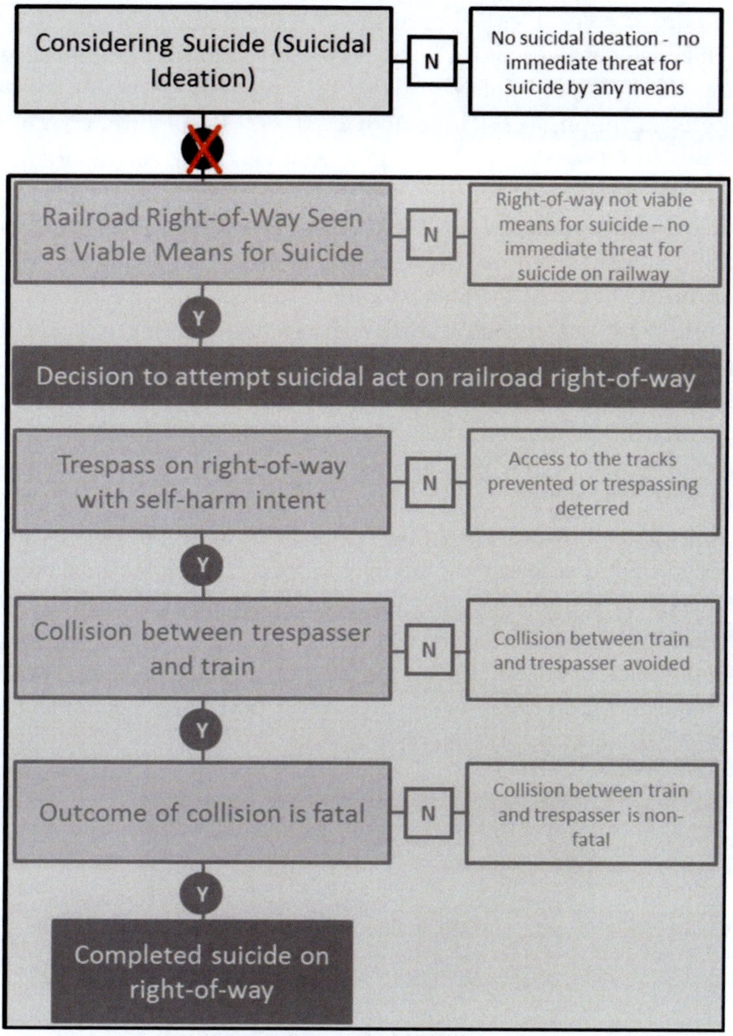

Figure 2. Countermeasures to Reduce Suicidal Ideation.

3.1.1. Blue Lights

Suicides on railroad rights-of-way occur almost twice per day in Japan; there were 682 railway suicides on passenger lines in 2009 (Matsubayashi, Sawada, and Ueda, 2012).[16] One way railroads in Japan have attempted to curb the number of suicides on the railroad rights-of-way is by installing blue Light-Emitting Diode (LED) lights at the ends of station platforms (Watanabe,

2011). Railroad companies believed that the addition of blue lighting would reduce suicidal behavior based on reported reductions in criminal behavior following the installation of blue lights on streets in Glasgow, Scotland, in 2000 and Nara, Japan, in 2005 (Dankova, 2011).[17] Results from the blue light installations in Glasgow and Nara have been anecdotal, as reports of crime reduction do not specify to what degree crime has been reduced, and no studies have been conducted to validate these claims or to explore alternative explanations (such as normal fluctuations in crime rate). Figure 3 shows a depiction of one of the LED lights on a Japan railroad station platform.

Despite a lack of empirical evidence that blue lighting has an effect on crime or suicide rates, media reports have speculated that the blue lights have a calming or relaxing effect which in turn may reduce suicide.[19, 20] This relaxing effect is thought to dissuade individuals who may be considering suicide. However, a study of the relaxation effects of blue light illumination on smoking behavior did not show any increased relaxation effects (Watanabe 2011). Relaxation, however, is not the only possible effect of blue lighting. For example, it is possible that the blue light casts an unfamiliar or unusual light on the passengers, creating an uneasy feeling that initially inhibits an individual's likelihood to commit a crime or jump on the right-of-way. Additionally, blue lights are often associated with police presence, which may suggest increased monitoring of the area. Over time these lights may become less unusual, reducing the initial effect.

Figure 3. Blue LED Lights in Japan Railroad Station Platforms.[18]

- **Current Use**
  In November of 2009, the East Japan Railway Company installed blue lights at each end of the platform at all 29 stations on the central train loop (Yamanote line) in Tokyo with the goal of reducing the number of suicides. Similarly, in 2010 the West Japan Railway company installed blue lights at 94 railway crossings. Currently, blue lights are not being used anywhere in the United States as a means to reduce suicides.
- **Evidence of Effectiveness for Rail**
  There is little scientific evidence to explain why blue light may work to reduce the suicide rate; however, railroad representatives have indicated that the blue lights are intended to have a calming effect on people.[21] The rate of suicides for one railway company in Japan was tracked from 2000 to 2010 at 71 stations, before and after the installation of the blue LED lights (Matsubayashi, Sawada, & Ueda, 2013). Blue lights were installed in 11 of these stations over the last 3 years of the study: 2008 (one station), 2009 (four additional stations), and 2010 (six additional stations). Researchers found that the introduction of the blue lights resulted in an 84 percent decrease in suicide across these stations. This estimate had a large confidence interval of 14–97 percent, due to a relatively small sample size, indicating a very unstable estimate. This study had several limitations. Only a small number of stations were sampled, and for relatively short periods of time, which does not allow us to account or adjust for any variation in suicide rates across the 11-year period, or to draw a conclusion as to the stability of these results.
  A subsequent examination of the blue light study data (Ichikawa, Inada, & Kumeji, 2013) revealed that 14 percent of all railroad suicides in Japan occur at night within railroad stations; only 28 percent of these suicide attempts occurred at the ends of the platform where the blue lights were installed. In Japan, more than half of the railroad-associated suicides occurred at night between stations (57 percent) as opposed to on the station platform. Blue lights installed in stations would therefore have limited impact on the overall prevention of railroad suicides in Japan. Ichikawa et al. (2013) further speculate that the blue lights may possibly influence individuals with suicidal ideation to consider other locations (away from the Right of Way (ROW) and specific times of day. Both studies of the blue lights in Japan concede that there has been no examination of the mechanism

by which the blue lights actually reduce the number of suicides. Without understanding how the blue light actually affects suicidal individuals, it is difficult to interpret any changes in suicide rates in a meaningful way.

- **Evidence of Effectiveness for Other Means**
  Blue light has been used outside of the railroad environment in a more clinical capacity to treat seasonal depression. Some researchers have shown that using narrow-band blue light can have significant antidepressant effects on individuals suffering from Seasonal Affective Disorder (SAD) (Glickman, Byrne, Pineda, Hauck, and Brainard, 2006; Strong, Marchant, Reimherr, Williams, Soni, & Mestas, 2008). However, these effects were noted after 3 consecutive weeks of 45 minute-long morning light exposure, periods of time that are longer than the average passenger would experience on a train platform. Light therapy (though not specifically blue light) has been shown in one study to be effective at reducing suicidal ideation (Lam, Tam, Shiah, Yatham, & Zis, 2000) though researchers have also shown that in rare cases, bright light may increase suicidality (Praschak-Rieder, Neumeister, Hesselmann, Willeit, Barnas, & Kasper, 1997). Even still, these effects have not been shown for blue light therapy specifically.
- **Evidence of Impact on Other Individuals**
  Blue lights were initially installed on the streets in Glasgow, Scotland, in 2000 to aesthetically improve the landscape. It was reported that this installation led to a decrease in crime rate. However, all reports of this reduction are anecdotal. None of these reports look at the effects of the lighting over a period of time long enough to rule out possible novelty effects of the blue lighting.[22]
  Blue light is believed to negatively affect human vision (Cole, 2005; Wu, 2004; Reme, Wenzel, Grimm & Iseli, 2003). The "blue light hazard," as it is often referred, has been identified as contributing to the development of macular degeneration (Ham, Ruffolo, Mueller, and Guerry III, 1980; Taylor, Munoz, West, Bressler, Bressler, and Rosenthal, 1990). Additionally, blue light has a strong effect on melatonin, a hormone that influences sleep and wake cycles (circadian rhythms).[23] It is unclear how increasing the amount of high intensity blue light exposure will affect the visual or sleep health of the passengers who frequent these train stations.

- **Feasibility of Railroad Implementation**
  Passenger Railroad Feasibility: Although it is conceivably possible for a passenger railroad to implement a blue light suicide mitigation program at specific locations, there is currently very little evidence that such an implementation would actually affect the rate of suicides on the railroad rights-of-way. We were unable to locate any studies that have looked at the long term effects of blue lights on suicide rates on the railroad rights-of-way. It is not currently known *why* such an implementation may be effective, and given the known hazards of blue light on visual health and sleep schedules, it is ill-advised to rush towards implementation of such a countermeasure. Additionally, more needs to be understood about the potential impacts of blue lights on train crews' ability to properly discern signals during different times of day or weather/visibility conditions. This countermeasure should be better understood before being implemented widely in the United States.
  Freight Railroad Feasibility: Such a countermeasure would not likely be possible for freight railroads to implement. This countermeasure requires blue lights to be positioned in specific locations where individuals are likely to wait for the train. While stations provide a common location where individuals gather, freight railroads do not have this same arrangement, so finding locations to install lights where they will impact a large number of individuals is difficult.

Summary Table. Blue Lights

Target Population	Benefits	Known Issues	Summary
Individuals on the train platform who have suicidal ideation	• Discreet • Passive way to reduce suicides	• High cost • Impact is not well studied • No established logic why reduction would occur • Potential long term harm to one's vision	Installation of blue lights on station platforms. The effect that blue lights have on an individual's psychological state is not well known. Systematic research is needed to understand the effects of these lights before any further implementation is merited.

3.1.2. Gatekeeper Training (Training to Identify Individuals Exhibiting At-Risk Behaviors for Suicide)

Gatekeeper training refers to training designated and authorized individuals to identify people who may be at a high risk for suicide. While doctors, psychiatrists and other clinical professionals interact with mental health patients are often trained to identify behaviors which may indicate suicidal intent, similar training could also be extended to trained railway personnel, or gatekeepers at stations when suicide attempts have previously occurred. Assuming doing so doesn't interfere with other safety-critical or customer service duties, these gatekeepers, who may be station staff, conductors, engineers, or other railroad personnel, would be trained to identify behaviors which may indicate suicidal risk, and to effectively attempt to intervene without endangering themselves or others.

- **Current Use**
  Gatekeeper training programs are currently implemented by some railroad carriers at stations in the United States.[24] In the United Kingdom (UK), there is a partnership between Network Rail and the Samaritans in the UK.[25] Initial investigations of the effectiveness of gatekeeper programs provided by the Samaritans have been conducted. Two training programs were developed: one aimed at front line staff to "boost skills and confidence in dealing with distressed individuals at railway locations," and a second aimed at "those supporting railway staff affected by trauma." Both training courses have been well received by attendees. Front line staff training focuses on suicide mitigation. The Samaritans trained over 4,000 railway industry staff in the first 3 years (2010–2012) of the gatekeeper program, and over 50 have already used the skills learned to help a passenger in need.[26] Not only can railway staff be trained to identify individuals exhibiting risk behaviors for suicide, but community residents can also be educated to reinforce suicide prevention. For example, in Barlaston, UK, when seven individuals were killed on the railroad rights-of-way over an 18-month period, the Samaritans teamed up with Network Rail to deliver a 6-hour course to Barlaston residents.[27] No evaluation of the effectiveness of this community training has been conducted to date.
- **Evidence of Effectiveness for Rail**
  Currently, there are no known empirical studies assessing the impact of gatekeeper training on suicides on the railroad rights-of-way. The

effectiveness of gatekeeper training depends on the individual's ability to identify risk based on observable behaviors and the institutional support of their employers. Therefore, existing research on behaviors that are common before suicide attempts on the railroad right-of-way can be very important indicators for the train and train station staff (e.g., Ratnayake, Links, & Eynan, 2007; Dinkel, Baumert, Erazo, & Ladwig, 2011). These behaviors may be used to identify those who are likely to use the right- of-way for a suicide attempt. For example, German Federal Police were surveyed about what behaviors they had witnessed prior to suicides on the railroad right-of-way and more than half had observed the dropping or leaving behind of personal belongings and an avoidance of eye contact; in addition, more than a third had observed erratic gestures or movements (Lukaschek, Baumert, & Ladwig, 2011). These types of behaviors could be considered behavioral signs and therefore become part of gatekeeper training. As part of the European Union's Reduction of Suicides and Trespasses on RAILway property (RESTRAIL) project, programs are currently underway to pilot-test potential intervention strategies based on observable behaviors at railway stations (Ryan, 2013).

- **Evidence of Effectiveness for Other Means**
  The majority of research regarding the effectiveness of gatekeeper training programs comes from the training of teachers, counselors, prison guards, and other individuals who play an active role in individuals' day-to-day lives (e.g., Rutz, von Knorring, & Walinder, 1992; King & Smith, 2000; Daniel, 2006; or Wyman, Brown, Inman, et al, 2008; Stuart, Waalen, & Haelstromm, 2003). For example, Stuart and colleagues (2003) found a significant increase in knowledge about suicide and skills for responding to suicidal peers after individuals went through a school-based peer training program. A meta-analysis of gatekeeper training studies showed that gatekeeper training had a positive effect on trainee attitudes, skills, and knowledge (Isaac, Elias, Katz, Belik, & Deane, 2009). Researchers believe that better knowledge, attitudes, and skills for identifying suicidal warning signs and intervening will lead to an increase in successful interventions. Nevertheless, none of the studies reviewed used a randomized controlled trial method; they were therefore unable to show an empirical effect on suicides rates.

- **Evidence of Impacts on Other Individuals**
  Gatekeeper training is unlikely to have an impact on individuals without suicidal ideation. As the goal of this countermeasure is to intervene directly with individuals who are displaying signs of distress, other passengers or trespassers are unlikely to be affected.
- **Feasibility of Railroad Implementation**
  Passenger Railroad Feasibility: We were unable to identify any gatekeeper training programs that have been empirically evaluated to determine if they are effective at reducing the number of suicides on the railroad rights-of-way; however, if implemented strategically, such gatekeeper programs may be able to help mitigate suicide incidents. Initial results from the collaboration between Network Rail and the Samaritans are showing some positive results. Between the initiation of training in 2010 and the end of the year in 2012, there had been anecdotal reports of at least 50 of 4,000 trained staff members using their training to intervene successfully. While more time is needed to better understand the long term impact of this training on the overall number of fatalities, the initial reports show promise for this countermeasure.[28] These gatekeeper programs are likely to be effective only for passenger operations where station staff can observe groups of individuals near the right-of-way.

Summary Table. Gatekeeper Training (Training to Identify Individuals Exhibiting Risk Behaviors for Suicide)

Target Population	Benefits	Known Issues	Summary
Individuals who have suicidal intent in a railroad station	• Relatively lower cost • Can use existing personnel • May be able to offer training to community	• Impact is not well studied • Stations are the most clear implementation site – harder for freight	The training of station staff (or others) to identify and intervene with individuals who appear to be exhibiting risk behaviors for suicide This holds promise and will only incur the costs of training personnel. Still impacts will only be seen on areas of track/stations which are actively monitored. Implementation on open track is less clear than in stations.

Freight Railroad Feasibility: Gatekeeper training programs are not likely to be effective for freight operations. Freight railroads do not have specific locations that can be monitored by trained gatekeepers, so a gatekeeper program which relies on both monitoring and immediate intervention may not be easily implemented. However, freight railroads, and passenger railroads as well, may observe reductions in suicide rates on the rights-of-way as a result of existing policies that encourage individuals to alert proper authorities when unauthorized persons are seen on or near railroad property. Additionally, mental health facilities located near railroad rights-of-way may be able to work with local community members, such as shop or restaurant owners, police, or residents of private residences, to share knowledge about how to identify at risk behaviors.

3.1.3. Public Awareness Campaigns (Suicide Focused)

A public awareness campaign is a systematic effort, through one or more mass media communication strategies, to alert the general population in a given area of a specific interest or concern. The public awareness campaigns discussed in this section promote awareness of suicide. These types of public awareness campaigns work in two ways. First, a public awareness campaign may provide information on where to find help for those who experience suicidal ideation and are considering suicide. Second, a campaign may inform the public of ways to identify behaviors that may indicate distress or the possibility that the individual is considering attempting suicide. Thus trained to identify risky behaviors, individuals can then report such activity to the appropriate authorities. An important consideration when developing a campaign is how the message will be conveyed to the intended audience. The wording used in public awareness campaigns or other publicly distributed material must be carefully considered (see Section 3.2.1 on Media Guidelines/Media Training for more information). A poorly worded public awareness campaign (e.g., one that emphasizes the lethality of trains) may have the unintended effect of "advertising" the railroad as a potential means by which an individual can end his or her life.

Note that the public awareness campaigns discussed in this section address suicide in general. While they may be implemented in a railway environment (e.g., a suicide help poster at a train station), the content of the campaign itself is about suicide and may not be specific to the railroad environment. Section 3.2.2 includes a discussion of public awareness efforts that focus on the railroad environment.

- **Current Use**

  Currently, there are no known public awareness campaigns in the United States that promote awareness of suicides on the railroad rights-of-way. In the UK, a public awareness campaign known as "We're in your Corner" was implemented through a partnership between Network Rail and the Samaritans that focuses on suicides on the railroad right-of-way.[29] The campaign aims to encourage middle-aged men, who make up approximately 80 percent of UK suicides on the railroad rights-of-way, to seek help for mental health issues.

  Though not suicide-specific, a variety of public awareness campaigns have been launched in the United States in an attempt to prevent trespassing on the right-of-way. For example, Operation Lifesaver, a non-profit organization, aimed to increase safety around railroad rights-of-way with the use of trespass-specific safety posters which can be found on their Web site (http://oli.org/education-resources/for-kids/safety-posters). This type of public awareness campaign is further discussed in Section 3.2 - Reduction of Perceived Viability of Railroad Right-of-Way as Means for Suicide.

- **Evidence of Effectiveness for Rail**

  Currently, there are no known public awareness campaigns in the United States that directly address suicides on the railroad right-of-way. Public awareness campaigns which target suicide in general or advertise help for those in distress are more common, although they do not typically discuss a particular means of suicide. Even the public awareness campaigns discussed above in the UK are not railroad-specific, though many of the posters are displayed in and around railway stations. There is no direct evidence in support of or against the potential of railway suicide-specific awareness campaigns to reduce suicides on the railroad right-of-way.

- **Evidence of Effectiveness for Other Means**

  Public awareness campaigns that focus on suicide have been implemented around the world. In a study investigating suicide rates in Regensburg, Germany, it was found that rates fell significantly during the time when publicity campaigns were active (Hubner-Liebermann, et al., 2010). This reduction in suicide rate was especially large for men, who were the focus of this particular campaign since they represented the portion of the population with the highest rate of suicide. However, the rates did start to climb towards the end of the study period despite the fact that the campaign was ongoing. In spite of this finding, the overwhelming evidence suggests that public awareness campaigns might be effective in certain settings as long as the audience to which the campaign is targeted is carefully considered.

In a meta-analysis of 15 known depression and/or suicide public awareness programs in 8 countries, a modest improvement in the public's knowledge about these topics was observed (Dumesnil and Verger, 2009). An increase in public knowledge about suicide or precursors to suicide, such as depression, is a large step towards identifying those near the right-of-way who may need help.

Little evidence has been found to date to indicate that public awareness campaigns about suicide lead to an increase in help-seeking behaviors or to a reduction in suicides. One program, Signs of Suicide (SOS), teaches adolescent students in a school setting about suicide and depression using videos and brochures. This program has proven effective in reducing suicide attempts and promoting helpful attitudes about depression and suicide (Aseltine & DeMartino, 2004). More research is needed to validate these and similar findings, to understand how aspects of programs that teach about suicide and depression might be used in a non-education setting, and to determine whether such efforts can be generalized to the railroad rights-of-way.

- **Evidence of Impact on Other Individuals**

  Railway suicide-specific public awareness campaigns are unlikely to have an impact on individuals without suicidal ideation. Public awareness campaigns are intended to reach the general population, which in this case includes far more than those individuals who exhibit risk behaviors for suicide on the rights-of-way.

  Although railway suicide-specific awareness campaigns are geared towards individuals with suicidal ideation, they may also help educate the general population about behaviors that indicate an individual is at risk for attempting suicide. This knowledge of risk behaviors would make train passengers more likely to intervene or alert an authority if or when they observe signs of distress in individuals around the right-of-way.

- **Feasibility of Railroad Implementation**

  Passenger Railroad Feasibility: Many public awareness campaigns already exist for *trespassing* on railroad rights-of-way. Concerns do exist; however, about how to implement campaigns without negatively impacting suicide rates (i.e. give the individual an idea of the means to attempt a suicidal act). As was done with crisis center signage, which is discussed in the following section, posters advertising the awareness campaign may be posted in railroad stations. However, stations are not the only location where a public awareness campaign may be effective. Campaigns may be implemented via radio, television, or through signage in communities through which the railroad passes. Passenger railroad carriers may consider working with local communities to implement such a campaign, as communities will likely have a shared interest in reducing suicides.

Summary Table. Public Awareness Campaigns (Suicide Focused)

Target Population	Benefits	Known Issues	Summary
Individuals in the general public who are considering suicide	• May discourage suicide in general, and not just rail • Involves the community in suicide prevention and identification efforts	• Not railroad specific • Campaigns that mention suicide and the railway may inadvertently advertise the right- of-way as a means for suicide	Launching a public awareness campaign aimed to inform the public about suicide. While not mentioning the railroad specifically, the campaigns may be presented to the public in the railroad environment. The goal of this countermeasure is to encourage those in need of help to seek out that help. It may also help to inform the public of warning signs of suicide. The wording of public campaigns should be considered carefully so as not to associate the railway with suicide.

Figure 4. Signage Used by Caltrain.[30]

Freight Railroad Feasibility: Because public awareness campaigns are intended to reach a wide audience, they will not only impact individuals considering suicide on passenger railway lines, but also freight railway lines. Freight railroads do not have stations where large numbers of passengers gather, so implementing a targeted campaign that will reach a large number of passengers exclusively is not as straightforward. However, as mentioned above, public awareness campaigns may be implemented outside of the immediate railroad environment. They may, for example, be implemented in local communities where citizens may exhibit risk behaviors for suicide attempts. The railroad carriers, FRA, or groups like Operation Lifesaver may advise local communities of hotspot locations where community campaigns may be targeted. Community- or State-run mental health organizations may also be valuable in developing an effective campaign.

3.1.4. Signage (Crisis Center)

The placement of signs to promote the accessibility of crisis hotlines has become an international effort, which includes Australia, New Zealand, Sweden, the UK and the United States. Signage has been placed on trains, in railway stations, or at other strategic locations along the right-of-way (e.g., grade crossings or known locations of past suicides or suicide attempts). These signs can vary greatly in message and design, but many direct the reader to contact a local crisis center if he or she is in need of help. Individuals considering suicide may choose to call this number before acting. An example of signage used by Caltrain, the commuter railroad service in the San Francisco Bay area, can be seen in Figure 4. Caltrain installed signage in stations, at grade crossings, and on fences along their right-of-way. Locations where signage is placed may be influenced by the number of past incidents (intentional or unintentional fatalities) at a location (e.g. hotspot), so areas of track near known hotspots, may be identified for signage installation. Similar signage has been implemented by other railroads (e.g., Toronto Transit, Massachusetts Bay Commuter Railroad, and several others), but those campaigns have typically limited signage to railroad stations based on the assumption that stations see the majority of pedestrian traffic and the signage will therefore reach the greatest number of people.

- **Current Use**
  Signage is currently implemented by passenger railroads worldwide and across the United States. Most signage efforts in the United States place signage in passenger stations where individuals using the railroad are most likely to see them; however, signs have also been posted in strategic locations along the right-of-way. As of August 2013, the following railroads had implemented signage campaigns which provide the telephone number of a local or national crisis center: Caltrain, Long Island Railroad (LIRR), Massachusetts Bay Commuter Railroad (MBCR), Massachusetts Bay Transportation Authority (MBTA), Metra, New Jersey Transit (NJT), and the Washington Metropolitan Area Transit Authority (WMATA). Outside of the United States, Toronto Transit (TTC) in Canada began using a signage campaign similar to those being used in the United States in June of 2011.[31] Signage on the Toronto Transit line is accompanied by a pay phone (provided by the Bell Mental Health Initiative, a multi-year mental health awareness initiative led by Bell Canada) where calls to the Crisis Link (the organization receiving crisis calls) can be made free of charge with a dedicated button on the phone.
- **Evidence of Effectiveness for Rail**
  The effectiveness of signage in reducing the number of suicides on the railroad right-of-way has not been thoroughly assessed. Only a portion of the railroads that have implemented signage have evaluated the use of the crisis center hotlines advertised on the signs. Due to the relatively small number of suicides that occur on a given railroad right-of-way in a given year, it may take several years to collect enough data to evaluate the effectiveness of such an intervention. Instead of assessing effectiveness solely through a count of suicides on the railroad right-of-way, some railroads have decided to include a unique crisis center telephone number on their signs so that they can work with the crisis center to better understand who is responding to the signage and taking advantage of the service. The Railroad Research Foundation (RRF) conducted a brief 9-month evaluation of the signage efforts of Caltrain, NJT, and LIRR. Although this short timeframe did not allow for rigorous evaluation, initial findings indicate that the unique crisis center numbers were called not only for suicide and crisis related issues, but also for unrelated problems such as inquiries about train scheduling (Appendix A includes more details about the findings of this study.)

If signage campaigns are implemented, railroads must decide whether a dedicated phone line should also be included. Although no research exists to address the necessity of a dedicated phone line with signage in the railroad environment, one investigation found that fewer than 5 of the 29 decedents included in their study were in possession of a cell phone at the time of death (Berman, et al., 2013). Although this is a small sample, it raises the question of whether the availability of a public telephone is necessary for this signage to be effective. Some may argue that a telephone is not necessary because individuals who attempt suicide on the railroad right-of-way may visit the site prior to the actual incident and therefore have an opportunity to see the number in advance. More research is needed to understand how individuals contact crisis center hotlines after reading railway station signage.

- **Evidence of Effectiveness for Other Means**

  Crisis hotlines are among the oldest suicide prevention countermeasures used in the United States (Litman, Farberow, Shneidman, Heilig, & Kramer, 1965). The use of hotlines has been shown empirically to reduce an individual's suicidal thoughts and, in some cases, prevent individuals from attempting suicide (Gould, Kalafat, Munfakh, and Kleinman, 2007). Research shows that not only are hotlines effective once reached, but also that individuals in need do reach out to crisis hotlines. For example, researchers observed a significant reduction in suicides at car parks in the New Forest region of the UK after signage promoting a crisis center (the Samaritans' national telephone number) was installed (King & Frost, 2005). The number of suicides fell from 10 per year to 3.3 per year after the signage was installed, while no significant increase was found in neighboring forest districts and car parks.

  Evidence gathered by monitoring nearby phones has been inconclusive regarding the effectiveness of signage and hotline use. Over a 2-year period, 30 of 39 potential bridge jumpers at the Mid-Hudson Bridge in Poughkeepsie, New York, called the crisis hotline from the bridge phone; only one of those individuals later died as a result of suicide by other means (Glatt, 1987). However, it was also found that five of the bridge jumpers leapt from the bridge to their death without using the available telephone. Signage and accompanying phones have been placed on a number of other bridges across the United States, including the Golden Gate Bridge in San

Francisco and the Tappan Zee Bridge in New York. Suicides have not been eliminated in those locations despite the presence of signage and accompanying phones, and follow-up studies have not been conducted to assess any potential reductions. In fact, in 2013, 46 individuals committed suicide by jumping from the Golden Gate Bridge; this was the highest yearly total in the history of the bridge.[32]

Research findings about bridge jumpers does not perfectly parallel individuals attempting suicide at the railroad station. Railroad stations are likely to have more people concentrated in a single area and are also likely to have people waiting around for a train.

- **Evidence of Impact on Other Individuals**
  Signage at railroad stations and along the right-of-way is likely to have little to no impact on individuals without suicidal ideation. The signage discussed in this section specifically encourages individuals in need of help to contact crisis centers. It is then up to that individual to reach out.
- **Feasibility of Railroad Implementation**
  Passenger Railroad Feasibility: Signage campaigns have been implemented by some passenger railroad companies around the United States. These campaigns are relatively low cost (if a direct phone line is not installed), which may make this option viable to railroads. However, the effectiveness of signage in reducing incidents on the railroad right-of-way has not been rigorously evaluated. Aside from the practical and logistical considerations, adding a telephone with direct access to the hotline may add significantly to the monetary cost of this type of countermeasure. When implementing its safety signage, Toronto Transit was able to help minimize costs to the railroad by partnering with Bell Mental Health Initiative who donated all of the phones for the effort. Individuals who choose to end their lives on the railroad right-of-way may be transient or may not have access to a cellphone, a fact which lends even more credence to the notion that a dedicated telephone is necessary for such signage to be effective. Additional research is needed to better understand the impacts of signage when paired with a phone compared with when presented alone.

  Freight Railroad Feasibility: Signage campaigns, though potentially effective in some settings, may be less straightforward for freight railroads to implement. Suicide-specific signage campaigns require individuals to see the sign in order to call the number on it. Unlike passenger railroads, which have stations where the passengers gather, freight railroads do not have clearly defined areas where individuals may gather and see a sign. Hotspot locations, or known shortcuts may be the best options for placement of signage in the freight railroad environment, although this would still not guarantee a positive impact for the railroad.

3.1.5. Training of Mental Health Providers

Mental health providers are often in a position to interact with and identify individuals at high risk for suicide. If mental health providers are in close proximity to the railroad rights-of-way, they may be in a position to identify behaviors from individuals specifically at risk for suicide attempts on the right-of-way. In a large longitudinal study (2000 to 2010) of eight Mental Health Research Networks health care systems, Ahmedani et al. (2014) reported that 83 percent had seen a health care provider, but only half had a mental health diagnosis, and only 24 percent had a mental health diagnosis within 4 weeks of their death. In this study, women were more likely to receive medical treatment in the year prior of those who have die by suicide than were men. Another study using data from 18 States from 2005 to 2010 revealed that approximately 29 percent of individuals received treatment before suicide (Niederkrotenthaler et al., 2014). This study reported that individuals with past suicide attempts—attempts involving poison or a history of depression and non-alcoholic substance abuse—had a slightly higher probability of receiving treatment before completing suicide. While the percentage of individuals receiving treatment for mental health problems close to the time of the suicide is not high, it provides some an opportunity for intervention. No data exists on how many individuals who attempt suicide specifically on the railroad rights-of-way are currently receiving treatment from mental health providers. A partnership between railroad carriers and mental health providers may increase awareness of suicides on the railroad rights-of-way among individuals in a position to provide needed care.

- **Current Use**

  We were unable to locate any information on collaboration between railroads and mental health facilities aimed at improving training to better identify individuals exhibiting risk behaviors for suicide on the railroad right-of-way. Such collaboration has been proposed but has yet to be acted upon (Mishara, 1999).

Summary Table. Signage (Crisis Center)

Target Population	Benefits	Known Issues	Summary
Individuals in a station or near train rights-of-way who may be considering suicide	• Inexpensive (without dedicated phone) • May impact suicide in general and not just rail	• Impact is not well studied • May require dedicated phone • Best implemented at stations – open track may be harder	Signage put up in stations or in targeted locations along the right- of-way with information about crisis center help lines Though the potential effects of crisis center signage on railway suicide rates are unknown, the use of anti-suicide signage as a suicide mitigation strategy holds promise. If implemented, railroads may consider working directly with the crisis center to track calls and monitor the use of the line.

- **Evidence of Effectiveness for Rail**
  Contact with mental health providers is not unusual as individuals who contemplate suicide often suffer from mental disorders (e.g., depression, bipolar disorder, etc.). Research shows that 53 percent of all suicides on the Dutch railway were receiving psychiatric care at the time of their death, including 49 percent who were in inpatient care (Van Houwelingen & Kerkhof, 2008). In the two U.S. studies mentioned previously (Ahmendani, et al, 2014; and Niederkrotenthaler, et al, 2014), about a quarter of the individuals received treatment for mental health disorders before the suicide. In a separate study of 129 suicides on the metro system in Montreal, Canada, between 1986 and 1996, 105 individuals were identified as having a mental illness. Of that number, 72 percent (76) were either residing in a treatment facility or had been prescribed psychotropic medication around the time of the suicide (Mishara, 1999). Eighty-one percent of railway suicide victims in Fyn County in Holland had been identified as psychiatric patients, compared with 38 percent among victims of suicide by other means (Lindekilde & Wang, 1985). In an epidemiological study of suicidal behavior on subway systems, researchers found that many of those attempting suicide experienced serious mental illness and had contact with mental health services

prior to the suicide attempts (Ratnayake, Links, & Eynan, 2007). Suicides on the London Underground tended to be clustered in stations adjacent to psychiatric facilities (Farmer, 1991). These studies indicate that substantial numbers of individuals who die by suicide on the railroad right-of- way and through other means have had contact with a mental health provider. It remains unclear exactly how the railroad industry can play a role in suicide interventions at the mental healthcare provider level. One possible option is to connect with providers in close proximity to the railroad to warn them about potential use of the right-of-way as a means to attempt suicide.

- **Evidence of Effectiveness for Other Means**

  As stated earlier, the ability to identify individuals exhibiting risk behaviors for suicide prior to an attempt is critical to reduce the number of suicide attempts that occur. Training to recognize behaviors that indicate high suicide risk has been shown to positively impact practitioner confidence in assessing and managing suicide risk. It has also been shown in many cases to result in the changing of care or clinical policies within a mental healthcare practice (Oordt, Jobes, Fonseca, & Schmidt, 2009). While not all individuals who attempt suicide will see a mental health provider, it is possible that many will.

  Railroad carriers may not be able to affect changes in mental healthcare training nationally, but may be able to contact facilities located near known hotspots or close to railroad rights- of-way. However, even non-rail specific policies which increase the ability of mental healthcare providers to identify warning signs of suicide have the potential to impact suicide rates by all means (including suicides on the right-of-way). On March 3, 2012, a bill which will require all mental health professionals to complete a training program in suicide assessment, treatment, and management at least once every 6 years (House Bill 2366, 2012) was unanimously passed in Washington State. This bill has not been in effect long enough to fully demonstrate its potential for impact; however, the passing of this bill may provide insight in the coming years into the benefits of improving suicide assessment, treatment, and management programs. If this mandatory training does lead to an increase in the identification and treatment of those considering suicide, it may pave the way for other States to follow suit and mandate such training.

- **Evidence of Impact on Other Individuals**
  The training of mental health providers is unlikely to have a significant impact on individuals without suicidal ideation. As this countermeasure focuses on educating professionals within the mental health community, the benefit will target individuals with suicidal ideation or intent.
- **Feasibility of Railroad Implementation**
  Passenger Railroad Feasibility: It may be possible for the passenger railroad industry to work with mental health providers serving a specific community located near railroad rights- of-way to inform them of the increased risk for suicides on the right-of-way. Training may specifically mention the railroad and warning signs specific to suicides on the railroad rights- of-way, but would also train mental healthcare providers to identify individuals exhibiting risk behaviors for suicide by any means. Ideally, if efforts to reduce suicides by all means focus on locations near the rights-of-way, suicides on the rights-of-way would likely also be reduced. Before investing in such an effort, railroads should take the time to understand if the proximity of a mental health facility does indeed increase the likelihood of suicide on the nearby right-of-way. It has yet to be proven that suicide incidents in the United States are to occur near mental health facilities than are accidental trespass fatalities, a factor which may impact the possibility of success for this countermeasure. Further, we were unable to locate any studies that specifically investigate the effects of providing additional training to mental health professionals and how this may help to reduce fatalities on the railroad rights-of-way.
  Freight Railroad Feasibility: If shown to be a potentially effective countermeasure, any railroad (or combination of railroads) could work with nearby mental health facilities to better identify those exhibiting risk behaviors for suicide on the railroad rights-of-way. However, as stated above, little evidence exists on how effective this type of countermeasure would be if implemented in the United States.

3.2. Reduction of Perceived Viability of Railroad Right-of-Way As Means for Suicide

Even if the countermeasures such as signage, hotlines, and mental healthcare provider interventions are effective, some individuals may never experience or come in contact with them. For example, individuals may never go to a train platform where the signage has been posted or they may never meet directly with a trained mental health services provider. For those individuals contemplating suicide, railroads may wish to dissuade them from choosing the railroad right-of-way as the means by which to attempt suicide. It may be possible to reduce the perceived viability of ending one's life on the right-of-way by either reducing the association between railroad and death or injury, or by reducing the perceived lethality of a train strike. For example, New York City's Department of Health and Mental Hygiene reported that 54 New Yorkers committed suicide on the subway system in 2011, with another 36 experiencing serious injuries that resulted from suspected attempts.[33] Figure 5 shows where, in the process outlined, countermeasures which would reduce the perceived viability of the railroad right-of-way as a means for suicide might be effective at reducing the number of suicides that occur on the railroad rights-of-way.

Summary Table. Training of Mental Health Providers

Target Population	Benefits	Known Issues	Summary
Individuals considering suicide who are receiving treatment from a mental health provider	• Mental health providers may be best equipped to help reduce ideation	• Impact not well studied • Unclear if railway suicide victims in the United States see mental health providers prior to action • Railroad carrier role is less clearly defined	Training of mental health providers near railroad rights-of- way to identify individuals exhibiting risk behaviors for suicide. This training is not specific to the railroad; however, if it can be shown that individuals who attempt suicide on the railroad are often seen by mental health providers, then the training of these providers to better identify individuals at risk may help to reduce the number of suicide attempts. The precise way that the railroads will work with the mental health providers has not been explored in the United States.

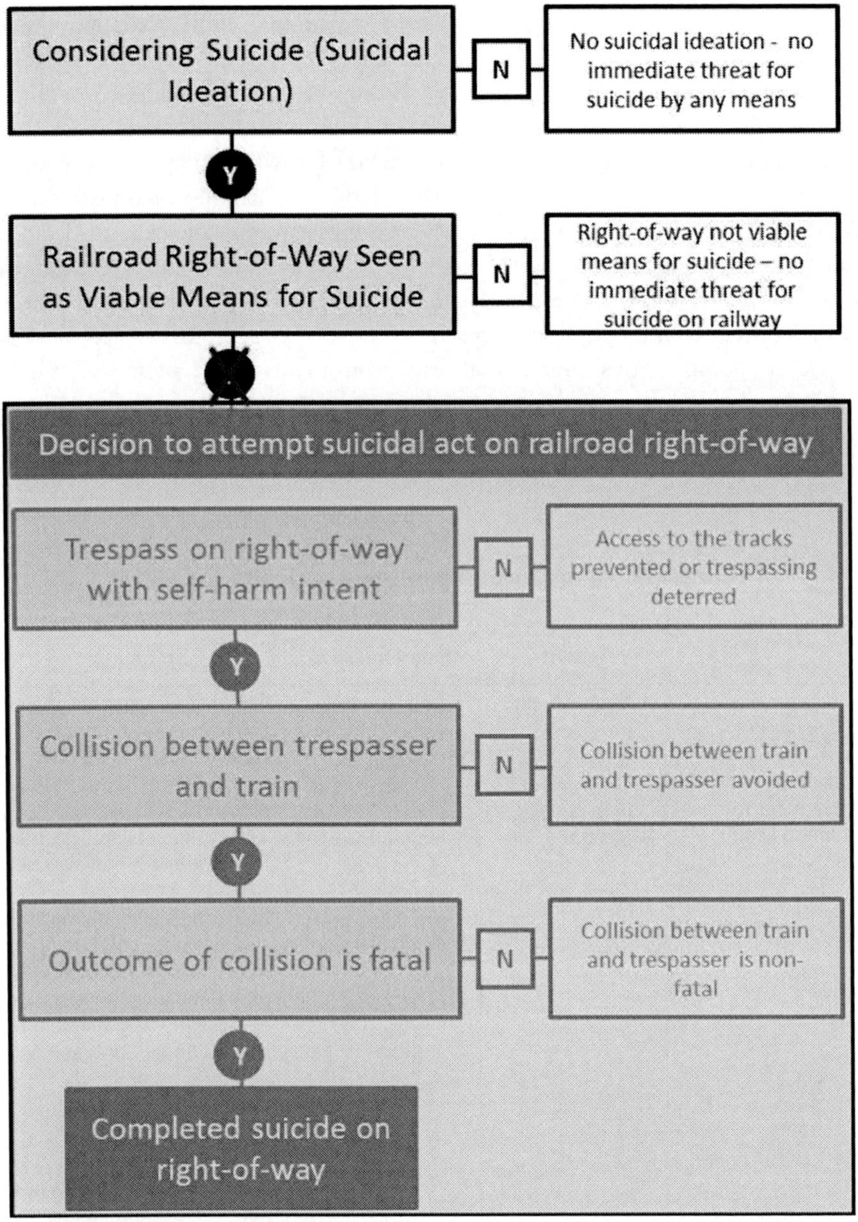

Figure 5. Countermeasures to Reduce Perception of Railway as Means for Suicide.

As with countermeasures to reduce or prevent suicidal ideation, the countermeasures are intended to reduce the perception of the railroad right-of-way as a viable means of suicide may have variable effectiveness. Individuals no longer seeing the railroad right-of-way as a viable method of suicide may still choose other means. In that case, the impact would be beneficial for train operators, bystanders, passengers, and so forth. We know that the effects of a trespasser strike or suicide on those who are immediately involved or who witness such an event can be profound, so any reduction in the number of incidents that occur on the railroad right-of-way is valuable (Gist, 2014).

Research has shown that if one means of suicide is prevented, individuals may not seek out other means to complete the act. One study found that 90 percent of individuals who had attempted suicide on the Golden Gate Bridge and survived did not go on to die of suicide by other violent means (Seiden, 1978). However, other studies report that the probability of completing suicide increases approximately 32 percent with each attempt (Leon, et al., 1990). Brådvik and Berglund (2011) reported that 46 percent of the people in their study have previously attempted suicide. In other studies, the median proportion of reattempts ranged from 2 to 10 percent (Christiansen & Frank, 2007; Leon, et al., 1990; Wang & Mortensen, 2006). Several factors such as living alone, neurobiological conditions, personality disorders, impulsiveness, and so forth were thought to contribute to the variability of reattempts. Brådvik (2013) reported that males were more likely to reattempt than were females. Postponing a suicide attempt by any means may give the individual an opportunity to rethink the intent to end his or her life, and also give intervening others an opportunity to observe risk behaviors. Studies that examine the intervening factors associated with reattempts may better assist railroads to better tailor their media messages. The countermeasures discussed in this section include:

- Media Guidelines/Media Training – Training the media to report suicides that occur on the railroad right-of-way in a way that does not encourage copycat behavior.
- Public Awareness Campaigns (Railroad-Focused) – Promoting awareness by the general public of the dangers of trains in a way that does not inadvertently advertise the railroad right-of-way as a potential means for suicide.

3.2.1. Media Guidelines/Media Training

The news media is believed to play a substantial role in influencing the suicide rate (e.g., Phillips, 1974; Niederkrotenthaler, Till, Kapusta, Voracek, Dervic, & Conneck, 2009; Sudak & Sudak, 2005). Media reports which use the term "suicide", especially in the title, and provide detailed information about the incident have been associated with increases in imitative suicide acts, or "copycat" behaviors. This phenomenon is known as the Werther Effect (Phillips, 1974). Phillips showed that an increase in suicides may occur following a widely publicized suicide; however, studies since then have been inconclusive, largely due to poor study designs. Even less is known about potential positive effects, a phenomenon referred to as the Papageno Effect, which the media could have on suicide rates (Niederkrotenthaler, Voracek, Herberth, Till, Strauss, Etzersdorfer, Eisenwort, & Sonneck, 2010).

- **Current Use**
  Media guidelines have been developed both in the United States and internationally to assist the press in reporting about suicide in a responsible way. The guidelines are intended to encourage journalists to educate the public about suicide prevention, help readers identify warning signs or likely causes of suicide, and reduce the likelihood of copycat incidents (the most up to date media guidelines are available at: http:// www.sprc.org/ sites/ sprc.org/ files/ library/ sreporting. pdf[34]). Current media reporting guidelines include recommendations such as not to include the word suicide in a headline; these guidelines are meant to keep viewers from possibly romanticizing suicide or idealizing those who take their own lives. Though guidelines for reporting exist, they are voluntary and there is little research about whether media outlets are following these guidelines when reporting on a suicide on the railroad right-of-way. Additionally, researchers have not investigated how the current media guidelines can be used with social media Web sites or blogs—places where many individuals in the United States obtain news and information.
- **Evidence of Effectiveness for Rail**
  Researchers have explored the various impacts of the media on suicide rates on the railroad rights-of-way. In the case of Robert Enke, a well-known German soccer player who died by suicide on the railroad right-of-way in Germany, the media was considered at least partially responsible for a rise in similar suicide incidents in the years following his death (Ladwig, Kunrath, Lukaschek, & Baumert, 2012).

An overall increase of 81 percent (from approximately 2.0 to 3.7 suicides per day on the railroad right-of-way) in the number suicides on the railroad right-of-way was found just after Enke's death when compared with similar, adjusted time periods from the years preceding it. Another study found that the number of suicides on the Vienna subway reduced dramatically by 75 percent (from nine suicides and ten attempts in the first 6 months of 1987 to two suicides and one attempt in the last 6 months of 1987) following an agreement by the media to abstain from reporting on cases of suicide (Sonneck, Etzersdorfer, & Nagel-Kuess, 1994). These reduced suicide rates remained stable for the next 3 years as well. A complete moratorium on reporting suicides on the railroad right-of-way, as was discussed in the Sonneck, et al. study, may not be possible or desired in the United States given the sheer number of different media outlets and the prevalence of social media within U.S. society. Still, if media outlets follow guidelines on how to report responsibly, a reduction in copycat incidents may be achievable.

- **Evidence of Effectiveness for Other Means**
  The media has been shown to have an impact on suicide rates for many different methods of suicide. A review was conducted of 56 studies to examine the effects of media on suicide rates (Sisask & Varnik, 2012) and 47 of these studies showed either an association between media coverage and increased suicidal behavior or media coverage as a deterrent that led to a reduction in suicidal behavior. Several of the studies included in this review also indicated effects based on age, with teenage (e.g., Kessler, Downey, Stipp, & Milavsky, 1989) and elderly, e.g., 65 and older, individuals being influenced more by the media (Stack, 1990). Some reports also found that the media may inadvertently "advertise" certain dramatic suicide methods including railroad and subway right-of-way suicide (e.g., Etzersdorfer, Sonneck, & Nagel-Kraus, 1992; or Kunrath, Baumert, & Ladwig, 2011), charcoal burning (e.g., Huh, Jo, Kim, Ahn, & Lee, 2009; or Chen, Liao, Teng, Tsai, Fan, Lee, & Cheng, 2010), and jumping from a high place (e.g., Reisch & Michel, 2005; or Yip, Fu, Yang, Ip, Chan, Chen, Lee, Law, & Hawton, 2006). There is also evidence that the media may be able to help reduce copycat attempts by including information about positive coping in adverse circumstances, though research on the effectiveness of this approach has not been conducted in the railroad environment

(Niederkrotenthaler, Voracek, Herberth, Till, Strauss, Etzersdorfer, Eisenwort, & Sonneck, 2010).

- **Evidence of Impacts on Other Individuals**
  Media guidelines are unlikely to have an observable impact on individuals without suicidal ideation or intent. The guidelines are designed to minimize the likelihood of copycat behaviors specifically among individuals with suicidal ideation. Individuals who are not thinking about or considering suicide will likely not be impacted by the suggested changes as many of the changes involve the removal of details or other minor changes to titles and images.
- **Feasibility of Railroad Implementation**
  Passenger Railroad Feasibility: Media guidelines exist for public reporting of suicide events in the United States. These guidelines are not specific to the railroad, but can likely be applied to suspected suicides on the railroad rights-of-way. It may be possible for railroad personnel to become familiar with or be trained on how to use these guidelines so that when they interact with the media, they can provide information that encourages responsible media reporting practices. In many cases, railroads already have policies for media interaction in place; however, a better understanding of how best to encourage responsible reporting may be necessary.

Summary Table. Media Guidelines/Media Training

Target Population	Benefits	Known Issues	Summary
The general public that reads, watches, or listens to the media	• Reduce the likelihood of copycat incidents and hotspots	• Cannot control social media • Unclear how to ensure that guidelines are adhered to	Provide media outlets with guidelines on how to report responsibly about suicides on the railroad rights-of-way. This countermeasure could reduce the number of copycat suicides likely to occur. The biggest challenges that remain are how to ensure that media outlets follow the guidelines and how to address the largely unregulated social media outlets.

Freight Railroad Feasibility: Media guidelines are likely to have similar impacts on the suicide rates of both passenger and freight railroads. Any suicide incident on freight or passenger rights-of-way may be reported by the local or national media. Many freight railroads already have protocols in place to discourage employees from speculating when speaking with the media. This approach encourages the media to wait for a coroner's verdict before reporting cause of death. In spite of these measures, irresponsible media reporting still occurs. The development of media guidelines which are easily understood, followed, and distributed may be a cost-effective solution to help minimize the number of copycat suicide incidents for all types of railroads.

3.2.2. Public Awareness Campaigns (Railroad-Focused)

Public awareness campaigns that attempt to reduce the overall number of suicides (not means- specific) are described above in Section 3.1.3 - Public Awareness Campaigns (Suicide Focused). However, it is possible that campaigns may be developed which focus more closely on incidents that occur on the railroad right-of-way. These railroad-specific public awareness campaigns may not focus directly on railroad right-of-way suicides, but impacts on railroad right-of-way suicides may be found through another campaign (e.g., a trespassing awareness campaign). Railroad- specific public awareness campaigns that focus on railroad right-of-way suicide may have counter-effective results if the message is not carefully crafted so as *not* to advertise the right-of- way as a viable means for suicide.

- **Current Use**
  Currently, a variety of public awareness campaigns exist to reduce the number of trespass- related incidents on the right-of-way. For example, a public awareness campaign may use billboards to discourage trespassing by implying that being struck by a train will result in death. Figure 6 shows an example of a billboard by the Tennessee Department of Transportation (DOT).

This type of messaging may be considered an effective way to discourage trespassing; however, it may also have the unintended effect of drawing the interest of an individual with suicidal intent to the railroad as a possible means to attempt suicide. Therefore, the campaign may ultimately reduce unintentional and/or accidental deaths, but increase intentional ones. There has not been any systematic evaluation of this campaign's effectiveness in reducing suicide or trespasser incidents.

Evidence of Effectiveness for Rail

Currently, there are no known nationwide public awareness campaigns in the United States that specifically address suicide on the railroad right-of-way. However, there are multiple public awareness campaigns that cover trespassing on the railroad right-of-way. For example, the billboard from the Tennessee DOT shown in Figure 6 or Brainy's World, which is a widely used public awareness campaign which advises people to "train your brain" to be smart at railroad crossings.[35] The Brainy's World campaign employs a poster and billboard campaigns as well as a mascot (a brain with arms and legs) that attends certain public events to spread awareness of railroad safety.

Figure 6. Tennessee Department of Transportation Railroad Crossing Billboard.

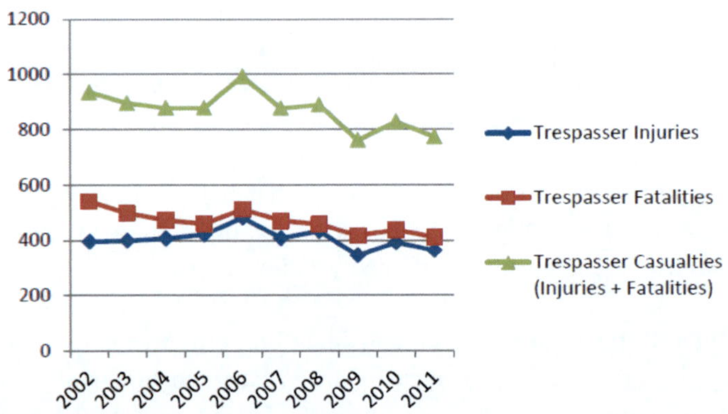

Figure 7. FRA Reported Trespasser Injuries and Fatalities.

Another way which the railroad industry spreads railroad safety information is through Operation Lifesaver Inc. (OLI), a non-profit organization that provides public education and promotes public awareness to prevent collisions, injuries and fatalities at highway-rail grade crossings or around railroad rights-of-way (the Operation Lifesaver website provides more information at www.oli.org/). However, trespasser casualties (both injuries and fatalities) have only shown a slight downward trend over the past 10 years, from 935 in 2002 down to 772 in 2011, with a peak in 2006 of 992 casualties (See Figure 7). Suicides had not been included in the FRA's reporting of trespasser casualties prior to June of 2011, so any potential effects of these campaigns on the rate of suicides on the right-of-way cannot be reliably determined. Anecdotally, conversations with several commuter railroad safety officials indicate that the rates of suicides have also remained constant or increased over the same timeframe[36].

Targeted outreach campaigns that are aimed to reduce trespassing may not always have a positive impact on both trespass and suicide rates. A 2013 news report from NJ.com (a web site for local New Jersey news) claimed that despite a recently launched safety initiative including warning signs and public service announcements, the number of fatalities on the NJ Transit system has increased. Especially of note, is that suicides reportedly comprise the majority of these fatalities (17 of the reported 23 fatalities through August in 2013 were suicides).[37] The reason for this spike has yet to be investigated thoroughly, but the timing of the increase (i.e., following highly publicized service announcements describing the lethality of trains) raises questions about the effectiveness of this campaign and its ability to reduce railway fatalities.

The notion that a train-person collision is nearly always lethal is also potentially misleading. A critical finding from the trespassing data shows that almost half of the individuals who are struck by a train survive that strike (see Figure 7). These data do not include fatalities that were determined by a coroner or medical examiner to be intentional acts of suicide, so they are likely somewhat skewed. However, research on suicidal acts on 23 subway systems around the world revealed a similar fatality rate of less than 60 percent for subway suicide attempts (O'Donnell & Farmer, 1992). This lower-than-expected fatality rate may be used as another potential deterrent for an individual considering the right-of-way as a means for suicide. An interpersonal-psychological perspective of suicidal behavior highlights a sense of *perceived burdensomeness* as one key factor leading to suicidality. Additionally, a *low sense of belonging/social alienation* and the *ability for self-harm* contribute to the likelihood of suicide (Joiner, 2005). A catastrophic injury to one's self would only increase the sense of burden. Knowing that death is *not* guaranteed may act to reduce the likelihood to attempt suicide in this manner. This, however, is only one working theory and many additional factors will also play into the decision to attempt to ends one's life.

- **Evidence of Effectiveness for Other Means**
  Public awareness campaigns specifically designed for the railroad industry are not intended for other means of suicide, but may nonetheless have beneficial outcomes in general. For information about other types of public awareness campaigns which are suicide specific, see Section I – *Public Awareness Campaigns (Suicide Focused)*.
- **Evidence of Impact on Other Individuals**
  Public awareness campaigns that are specific to suicides on the railroad rights-of-way are unlikely to have a noticeable impact on individuals without suicidal ideation or intent. These public awareness campaigns target a specific audience and anyone outside of that audience will not be greatly impacted.

Summary Table. Public Awareness Campaigns (Railroad Focused)

Target Population	Benefits	Known Issues	Summary
Individuals in the general public who may interact with the railway system	• Discreet way to reach suicidal population • May impact suicides as well as trespassers	• Impact is not well studied • Wording of campaign may increase suicides if not careful	Launching a public awareness campaign that will inform the public about dangers around the railroad rights-of-way. While not mentioning suicide specifically, the campaigns may be presented to the public in a way that may have an impact on suicides as well. The goal of this countermeasure is to identify ways to modify existing trespassing campaigns so that they do not inadvertently advertise the right-of-way as a means for suicide. Ideally these campaigns would bring down all fatality rates.

- **Feasibility of Railroad Implementation**
  Passenger Railroad Feasibility: Public awareness campaigns currently exist for trespassing on railroad rights-of-way, but none were found that focused on suicides on the railroad rights-of-way (though a similar campaign for suicide in general is discussed in Section 3.1.3). One major concern with current trespasser campaigns is that they focus on the lethality of trains, and they only address those at risk for trespass and not suicide. One solution may be to alter existing trespasser campaigns to define the danger of trespassing in terms of a risk of great injury instead of death. This type of messaging may have the same effect on trespassers while also communicating that lethality is not guaranteed for potential suicide attempters. Passenger railroads may be best equipped to implement smaller-scale public campaigns such as poster campaigns on trains or at stations.
  Freight Railroad Feasibility: Any public awareness campaign which reaches the general public will have an effect on both freight and passenger operations. As such, the feasibility for freight railroad implementation is very similar to that of passenger operations, though freight railroads do not have stations where large numbers of passengers will gather. Instead, freight railroads that wish to implement a public awareness campaign may consider alternative methods, such as billboards, placement at or near hotspots, or other widely viewable media options.

3.3. Prevention of Access to the Right-of-Way

The next set of countermeasures is designed to stop an individual who has suicidal ideation and sees the right-of-way to be a viable means for suicide. If an individual with suicidal intent is successfully deterred from physically accessing the right-of-way, then the potential suicide attempt is averted. Figure 8 below illustrates where this set of countermeasures would be implemented on the schematic.

An individual with suicidal ideation who believes that the railroad right-of-way is a viable option for suicide must first enter the railroad right-of-way. By deterring an individual from physically accessing the right-of-way, you prevent the train from striking them.

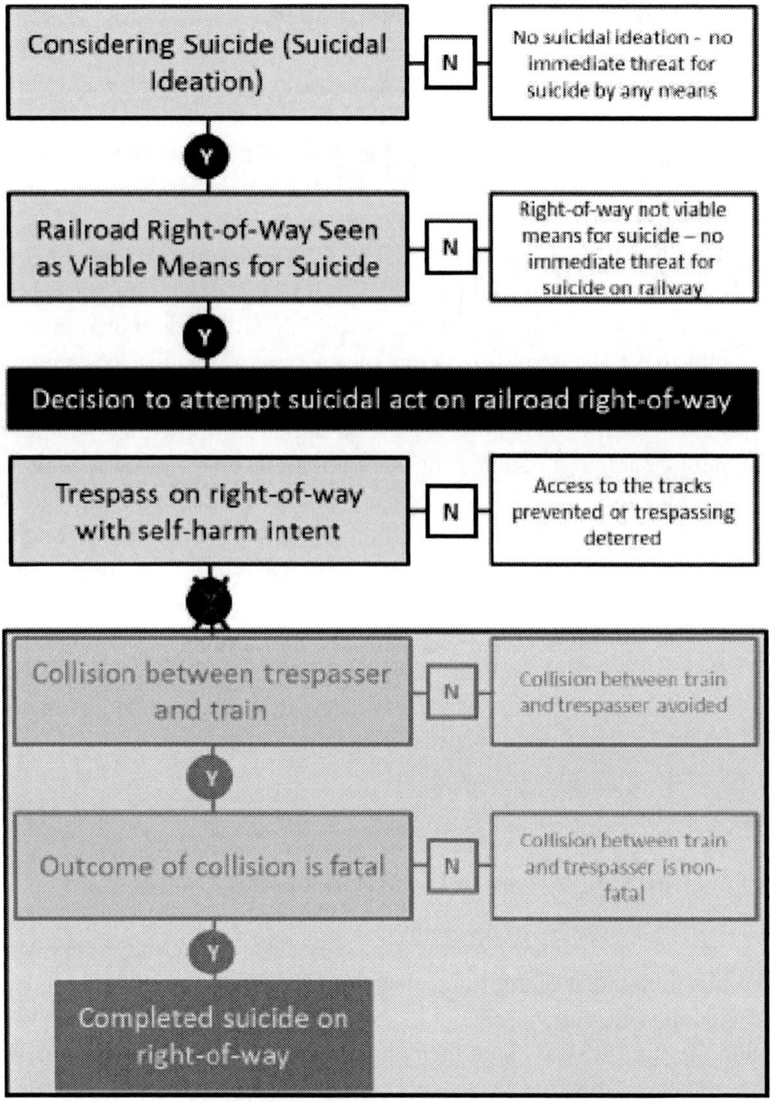

Figure 8. Countermeasures to Restrict Access to the Right-of-Way.

With roughly 140,000 miles of mainline railroad track in the United States, restricting access to the entire right-of-way is not feasible from an industrial engineering and architectural perspective. Even if restricting access to the entire right-of-way was not cost prohibitive, it is impossible and illogical to restrict access to more than 250,000 highway-rail grade crossings across the United States, because the highway-rail grade crossings must remain unrestricted to allow pedestrians and vehicles to pass over the rights-of-way. As a result, the countermeasures discussed in this section include:

- Means Restriction/Fencing – Directly restrict access to the rights-of-way through fencing or other similar efforts, such as bushes or sound attenuating walls.
- Platform Edge Doors (PEDs) – Installation of automatic doors in railway stations which remain closed, restricting access to the tracks rights-of-way until the train has completely entered the station and the train doors open.

3.3.1. Means Restriction/Fencing

Fencing is one way to physically impede or restrict an individual's access to the railroad right-of- way. While it is not reasonable to install fencing along the entire right-of-way (due to the vast nature of the United States railroad system and necessary access points such as grade crossings), it may be possible to target certain high-risk areas for fencing as discussed in Belgium, where research has focused on installing countermeasures at identified hotspots (Andriessen & Krysinska, 2012).

There is debate, however, about how effective targeted fencing may be. For example, a 2008 FRA fact sheet states "In general, the widespread installation of fences along railroad right-of- way is impractical, and many previous attempts to use fencing on localized basis have been ineffective as those determined to trespass have vandalized, damaged or otherwise destroyed the structures to restore the unfettered access they were previously accustomed to."[38]

If fencing is to be effective in targeted high-risk areas (e.g. hotspots), it is important to choose a type of fencing which ensures that the fence's integrity is not undermined by vandalism. Figure 9 shows three different types of fencing. Panel A shows how low-quality or less-strong fencing can be damaged to make trespassing easy. In this case, trespassers may disregard the fencing and cut or trample it. In contrast, Panels B and C display new types of fencing which are resistant to tampering and difficult to climb over. A thorough discussion of possible fencing types can be found on the Federal Highway Administration (FHWA) website: (http://www.fhwa.dot.gov/environment/recreational_trails/publications/rwt/fencing.cfm).

Figure 9. Examples of Fencing Along Railroad Rights-of-Way.

- **Current Use**

  Fencing is widely used throughout the United States to restrict access to the right-of-way; it is often used strategically in places where trespassing is a known problem. Additionally, fencing is often used at stations between parallel sets of tracks to discourage pedestrians from trying to access another platform by crossing over the right-of-way. A primary concern with fencing is vandalism. Fencing is often cut by vandals in areas where trespassing is common so that they can illegally cross the right-of-way without having to travel to a designated pedestrian crossing are, such as a grade crossing. There are a variety of fencing materials available, some which are more resistant to individuals trying to cut through it. The fencing options discussed on the FHWA website listed above include the following (note that a concrete wall is also discussed on the site):

  - Type I: Picket Fence – For use where trespassing is not much of a problem. It serves as a reminder to stay off the tracks.
  - Type II: Post and Cable – For use where trespassing is not much of a problem. It demarcates railroad property, but does not offer anti-trespassing features.
  - Type III: Chain-Link – For keeping unauthorized personnel off the tracks at relatively low cost. May not be appropriate for rural areas with no history of trespassing or for areas with high trespassing rates since it is very easy to cut and vandalize.
  - Type-IV: Vinyl-Coated Chain-Link – Similar to Type III, but with plastic or wood battens woven into the chain-link providing additional wind and visual buffering.
  - Type-V: Israeli-Style Steel Fence – For use when aesthetics or wind and visual buffering are not needed. This fencing is more expensive than chain-link, but is difficult to vandalize and climb. It is also relatively easy to repair if cut.

- Type-VI: Wrought Iron Picket Fence – For use where there is a history of trespassing. Virtually impossible to cut and difficult to climb. There is a high initial cost, but this type of fencing is vandal-resistant, so maintenance costs are likely lower.

To date, there have been no efforts to evaluate fencing's effectiveness in preventing suicides inside the United States. However, if a fence is capable of preventing access to the tracks, then it will very likely reduce the possibility of suicide attempts within that section of track.

In addition to fencing along the right-of-way, fencing on station platforms can be used to prevent suicide. Network Rail, which is located in the UK, limits access to portions of the platform where fast moving trains will pass through without stopping by using mid-platform fencing, as shown in Figure 10.

- **Evidence of Effectiveness for Rail**
  We have been unable to identify any studies which have investigated the effectiveness of fencing to deter suicides on the railroad right-of-way in the United States. Additionally, since the exact locations and installation dates of most fencing around the country are not tracked for evaluation (at least publicly); it is not known how existing fencing has affected trespasser fatalities.

Figure 10. Example of Mid-Platform Fencing at a Station in the UK.

In the UK, the majority of the right-of-way is fenced, generally due to older laws which were meant to keep livestock from obstructing railroad traffic.[39] In the United States, such widespread fencing may not be possible due to the nation's extensive railway system (over 13 times more track).[40] However, despite having relatively few trespasser related fatalities in the UK, the number of suicides per year is still quite high. This may bring into question whether fencing, and more specifically, the types of fencing used in the UK (which may not be robust enough if the fenced-in portions of the track are designed to prevent livestock access), may prevent both unintentional deaths and suicides on the railroad right-of-way.

- **Evidence of Effectiveness for Other Means**
  The methods of mean restriction can change depending on the method of suicide that is being prevented. For suicides on the railroad right-of-way, fencing may be effective means to restrict access to the right-of-way. Means restriction has proven effective for other means of suicide. For example, barriers on the Grafton Bridge in Auckland, New Zealand were shown to effectively lower suicide rates on that bridge (Beautrais, Gibb, Fergusson, Horwood, & Larkin, 2009). Removing suicide prevention barriers from the bridge in 1996 resulted in an immediate five-fold increase in suicide jumps from the bridge. The barriers were replaced in 2003 and no documented suicides occurred between 2003 and 2006. Less directly comparable, but still another example of means restriction would be changing the packaging of analgesics to blister packets in the UK, which was found to have reduced the number of analgesic related suicides (Hawton, 2002).
- **Evidence of Impact on Other Individuals**
  We have been unable to identify any studies which have investigated the effectiveness of fencing to deter railway trespassing in the United States. However, the fencing is not specific to suicide prevention and therefore may be expected to have similar impacts on trespassing and suicide. The purpose of fencing is to restrict access to the right-of-way which, if effective, would reduce both potential trespassers and suicide attempts.
- **Feasibility of Railroad Implementation**
  Passenger Railroad Feasibility: Currently, fencing is widely used by passenger railroads to keep trespassers off of the railroad right-of-way. While fencing off the entire right-of-way is not feasible, it may

be possible to fence areas on the railroad right-of-way which have been identified as a high risk for suicide. More research is needed to determine where these high risk regions of track are and why certain regions of track see temporary increases in suicide activity. Railroads must also consider the durability and the cost of maintenance, especially if less durable fencing options are used. Weighing the costs (including both upfront costs and maintenance costs) as well as benefits may help railroad carriers to determine if fencing is a viable option and which types of fencing will be most cost effective in the long term. Railroads may be able to share the cost of installing or maintaining fencing along the right-of-way with local communities. Additionally, mid-platform fencing may be considered for stations where trains pass through at high speeds.

Freight Railroad Feasibility: Freight railroads, like passenger railroads, may use fencing to help keep trespassers off of the rights-of-way. In some cases, freight and passenger railroads may share the same rights-of-way, so installation and maintenance costs may be shared between railroads and with local communities. Due to the expansive nature of most freight railroads, they will need to carefully monitor the locations of incidents and near misses in order to identify specific hotspots where fencing may be useful.

Summary Table. Means Restriction

Target Population	Benefits	Known Issues	Summary
Individuals with suicidal intent who are attempting to gain access to the right-of-way	• Physically limits track access • New fencing is more difficult to vandalize or climb • Impacts on both suicide and trespass	• Impact is not well studied • Cost of high quality fencing is high up front • Low quality fencing can be easily vandalized • Impossible to fence entire right- of-way	Restricting access to the rights-of-way through fencing, shrubbery or another means. Using fencing may reduce trespassing and suicide fatalities, especially when used in targeted hotspot areas. However, less durable fencing options are easily vandalized, which would allow access to the right-of-way. Both up-front costs of a fence and maintenance costs must be accounted for when choosing a fencing option.

Figure 11. Full (Panel A) and Partial (Panel B) Length Platform Edge Doors.[41]

3.3.2. Platform Edge Doors (PEDs)

Platform Edge Doors (PEDs), also known as Platform Screen Doors (PSD), are doors that open after a train has completely entered a station and prevent individuals from entering the right-of- way before a train arrives. Most PEDs are made of glass, and they may extend the full length of the right of way at the station to completely seal off the entrance until the doors open, or the PED may also partially cover the right of way, acting like a fence with open space above it. The example in panel A of Figure 11 is a full length PED from the Canary Wharf Station in London, UK, the only station in London which currently uses PEDs. Panel B is an image of a partial PED from the Sunny Bay Station on the Disneyland Resort Line in Hong Kong, only one of few stations to only use partial PEDs.

- **Current Use**
  PEDs have been installed at railroad stations around the world, including the UK, Hong Kong, France, Japan, Singapore, and even in the United States on Airport Transportation Systems such as the railway at O'Hare International Airport in Chicago, Illinois; Hartsfield- Jackson Atlanta International Airport; and Washington Dulles International Airport in Washington, D.C. In many cases, the PEDs are installed to provide additional control over the heating and/or cooling of the station (i.e., the PEDs minimize the warm/cool air that escapes down the right-of-way) or keep debris from landing on the right-of-way. However, PEDs also control passengers' ability to access the right-of-way. In Mexico City, Mexico (Federal District) PEDs were installed in two stations in 2011. While security was the primary reason for their installation, it was not their only function;

PEDs were also believed to assist in preventing suicide. Other railroads have installed PEDs with suicide and trespass prevention as a goal. For example, the Hong Kong Mass Transit Railway (MTR) Corporation, the Paris Metro, and the underground stations of the Copenhagen Metro, among many others, all have PEDs. PEDs are listed as an evidence-based suicide prevention program in this 2010 report.

- **Evidence of Effectiveness for Rail**
  The implementation of PEDs on an underground railway network in Hong Kong (known as the Mass Transit Railway or MTR) was designed as a cost-savings effort to keep cool air in the subway stations. However, the PEDs were also found to have a clear effect on suicides (Law, Yip, Chan, Fu, Wong, & Law, 2009) in a study of the impact on suicide rates of the MTR PEDs that provides the largest amount of empirical evidence to date. The installation of the PEDs resulted in an 82% (38 down to 7) reduction in suicides on the MTR lines in the five years following the installation of the PEDs (2003-2007) when compared to the five years prior to the installation of the PEDs (1997-2001). There was no evidence of displacement (i.e. the reduction in suicides in the stations with PEDs was not coupled with a significant increase in other parts of the track or on other lines). The nearby Kowloon-Canton Railway (KCR), which operates a rail link between Hong Kong and nearby suburban regions, did not install any PEDs and saw no change in suicide rates during the same time period (13 suicides from 1997-2001 and 15 suicides from 2003-2007).
- **Evidence of Effectiveness for Other Means**
  There are no other countermeasures for other means of suicide which PEDs since they are specifically designed for a railroad environment. They restrict the means in much the way fencing does, however, they work in tandem with the train such that access to the train can be temporarily granted after the train has arrived.
- **Evidence of Impact on Other Individuals**
  PEDs will affect all railroad passengers in the same way. An individual with suicidal intent will experience the same barrier between them and the right-of-way that any other passenger would. The PEDs will prevent individuals with self-harm intent from accessing the right-of- way, but they will also deter inadvertent falls onto the right-of-way. Passengers under the influence of drugs or alcohol may inadvertently fall onto the right-of-way and adding a

barrier between the platform and the right-of-way may minimize the occurrence of such events. Additionally, a barrier between the platform and the right-of-way will make it more difficult for items to fall onto the tracks, thus reducing the possibility that a passenger may willingly enter the right-of-way to retrieve an item.

- **Feasibility of Railroad Implementation**
  Passenger Railroad Feasibility: Installing PEDs in passenger railroad stations in the US is promising, but it may be costly. Additionally, the majority of rights-of-way suicides in the United States take place on open track where PED installation is not possible, which limits the utility of this countermeasure. However, if specific railway stations exhibit higher than expected rates of suicides, small-scale implementations may be worthwhile. Little to no displacement effects (i.e., individuals seeking out nearby unrestricted access to the right-of-way) have been reported (Law, et al, 2009), so it is probable that instillation of PEDs at one station may not result in an increase in adjacent stations. Finally, PEDs have only been used in indoor settings where environmental debris and weather are not typically factors, and these issues must all be considered before PEDs are installed outdoors.

Summary Table. Platform Edge Doors

Target Population	Benefits	Known Issues	Summary
Individuals with suicidal intent on a train station platform	• Completely restricts access to right-of-way in the station • Can also keep individuals from falling onto right- of-way • Can also keep debris off right- of-way and manage temperatures in station	• Very high cost • Some existing stations may not support added weight • Only effective at stations	Installation of Platform Edge Doors (PEDs) which block access to right-of-way at stations until the train has stopped in place at which point access to the train is granted. PEDs are likely to be effective. However, they are extremely costly and can only be implemented at stations.

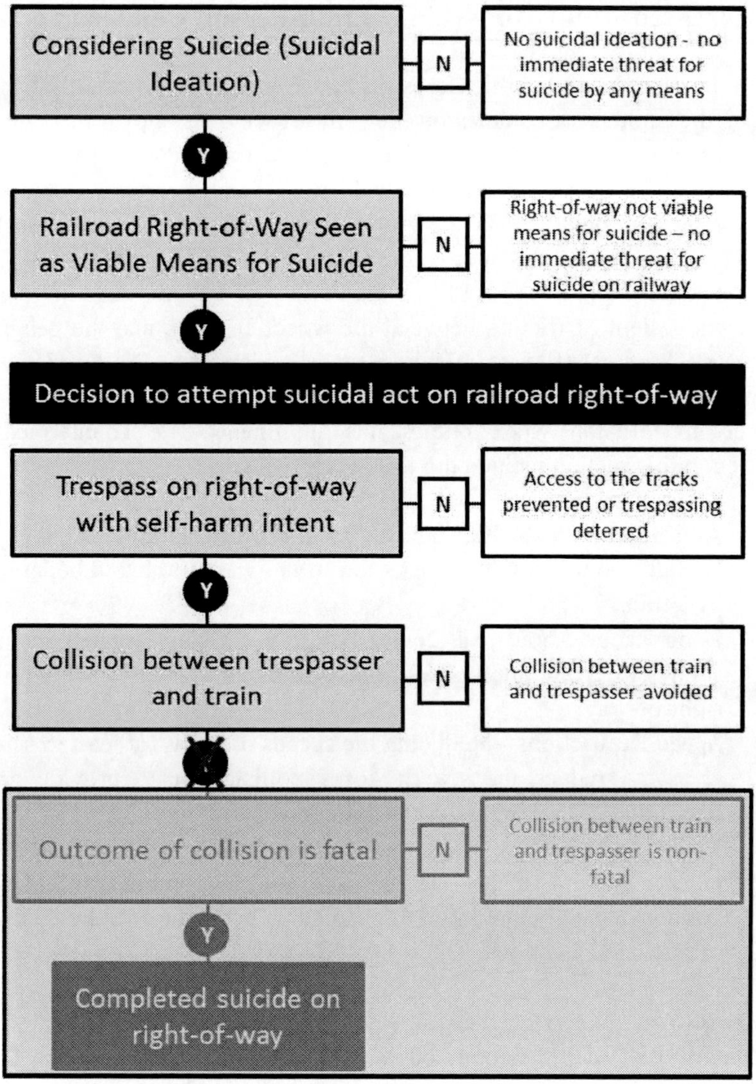

Figure 12. Countermeasures to Reduce Likelihood of Train-Person Collision.

Freight Railroad Feasibility: The installation of PEDs is not possible for freight operations. PEDs require a station where individuals gather to enter the train. Without a fixed location like a station, installation is not possible.

3.4. Increased Ability to Avoid a Train-Person Collision

The next set of countermeasures discussed examines potential means for reducing the number of suicides on the right-of-way. As shown in Figure 12, these countermeasures are designed to increase the chances that imminent collisions with trespassers will be avoided.

Once an individual is on the right-of-way and a train is approaching, avoiding a train-person collision is a time critical event. The braking distance of a train is long and depends on a wide variety of factors, including: speed, weight, coefficient of friction between the wheel and rail, and the geography of the track etc. (Barney, Haley, and Nidandros, 2001). However, countermeasures have been proposed which may decrease the probability of a train-person collision when one seems imminent. The countermeasures discussed in this section include the following:

- Anti-Suicide Pits – Elevated tracks in railway stations which provide enough room below the tracks for an individual to avoid being struck by a train.
- Long Range Acoustical Device (LRAD) – Using targeted acoustical sounds to create an unpleasant setting for individuals on the railroad right-of-way.
- Speed Restrictions – Reducing the speeds of trains (at least in selected areas) to reduce the severity of a collision or to provide greater likelihood of braking before the collision.
- Track Surveillance – Continuous observation of the right-of-way either by individuals, technology, or a combination of both. Authorities will be notified of suspicious behavior or individuals seen in restricted locations.

3.4.1. Anti-Suicide Pits

Roughly half of the stations on the London Underground in the United Kingdom (UK) that are deep underground, a term used but not defined by the researchers, have pits beneath the track (Coats and Walter, 1999). These pits, which are approximately three feet deep and were originally built for drainage, are known as “anti-suicide pits” and they help prevent death or serious injury to individuals who fall or jump onto the right-of-way. Individuals who accidentally fall onto the right-of-way or who have second thoughts about their actions can use the anti- suicide pit to avoid being struck by the train (by lying underneath the train in the pit). The space also makes it difficult for individuals to be pulled underneath the train where additional injuries can occur. Instead, they are knocked below the train into a space where the train can no longer strike them.

- **Current Use**
  Anti-suicide pits are currently being used in the United Kingdom's London Underground. This countermeasure is only present in a portion of the stations that are deep underground. A review of the literature did not reveal why those Underground stations were chosen to receive anti-suicide pits. Other systems, such as the Bangkok Skytrain and the Paris Metro, are thought to have anti-suicide pits; however, less has been written about these installations.
- **Evidence of Effectiveness for Rail**
  Between January 1996 and March 1997, fifty-eight individuals fell or jumped under a train at a London Underground station (Coats and Walter, 1999). Thirty-two of these incidents occurred in a station with an anti-suicide pit and 14 of them resulted in a fatality (fatality rate of 44 percent), while stations without anti-suicide pits had 21 incidents and 16 of them resulted in a fatality (fatality rate of 75 percent). Before any conclusions about the effectiveness of anti-suicide pits for preventing suicide can be made, these findings must be investigated further. First, it is unknown how many of the incidents were intentional. The suicide pits may be effective at preventing death or possible injury in the case of an accidental fall, while suicide-oriented incidents could be unaffected. A more thorough investigation into the types of incidents and the fatality rate is needed before meaningful conclusions can be drawn about the suicide pits effectiveness to reduce suicides at railway stations.
- **Evidence of Effectiveness for Other Means**
  Anti-suicide pits are specific to a railroad environment and as such, there is no direct evidence for its effectiveness in preventing other means of suicide. The closest parallel to the anti-suicide pits would be nets which have been installed on bridges or tall buildings to catch individuals attempting suicide or who accidentally fall. Like the suicide pits, these nets act to prevent the individual from completing suicide after an attempt has been made. After nets were installed on the Clifton suspension bridge in Bristol, England in 1998 there was an immediate reduction in suicide fatalities (50 percent reduction) and no subsequent rise in nearby areas (Bennewith, Nowers, & Gunnel,

2007). However, studies over a longer timeframe may be necessary to assess the long term effectiveness of these nets. Net systems have been proposed or implemented in locations in the US, such as an implementation in Ithaca, New York[42] and a proposal for the Golden Gate Bridge in San Francisco, California.[43]

- **Evidence of Impact on Other Individuals**
  Anti-suicide pits may have an impact on both those intent on suicide as well as individuals who inadvertently find themselves on the right-of-way (e.g., after a fall or trespassing onto right-of-way to retrieve a dropped item). While anti-suicide pits cannot prevent an individual from being struck by a train they do provide individuals who find themselves on the right-of-way with a means to avoid being struck. In fact, individuals who are on the right-of-way and have a desire to not be struck may find the anti-suicide pits most helpful.

Figure 13. Anti-Suicide Pits on the London Underground, UK.

- **Feasibility of Railroad Implementation**
  Passenger Railroad Feasibility: Anti-suicide pits may assist individuals who inadvertently find themselves on the railroad right-of-way at a station. In these cases, individuals can safely lay below the train in the suicide pit as the train passes above them. The anti-suicide pits provide one last opportunity to avoid being struck if the individual realizes after entering the right-of-way that they no longer wish to end their life. Installing anti-suicide pits on an existing railway network where the railroad infrastructure has already been constructed may be costly; however, anti-suicide pits may be worth considering when constructing new stations.
  Freight Railroad Feasibility: Since anti-suicide pits are specific to stations where the tracks can be temporarily elevated off the ground, they cannot be employed in the freight railroad environment.

Summary Table. Anti-Suicide Pits

Target Population	Benefits	Known Issues	Summary
Individuals who enter the right-of-way at a station	• Provide last-minute way to avoid contact with train once on right-of-way • May reduce fatal incidents by knocking into pit below train instead of under the wheels	• Impacts not well known • Very high cost to modify existing stations • Only effective at stations	A gap underneath an elevated track in a station that provides a location for a person to avoid contact. Anti-suicide pits provide a last minute place for an individual to escape a collision with a train. Additionally, in the event of a train-person collision, the individual is less likely to be taken under the wheels of the train where additional injury is likely to occur. Anti-suicide pits are not common and evidence of impacts is weak.

3.4.2. Long Range Acoustical Device (LRAD)

The use of non-lethal acoustic devices to dissuade people from staying on the right-of-way has been discussed by individuals involved in or familiar with the railroad industry.[44]

The proposed use would be for the train driver to use High Intensity Directed Acoustic (HIDA) devices such as the Long Range Acoustic Device (LRAD) to deliver a burst of sound (up to 130db) directly at an individual(s) on the right-of-way. Unlike a train horn, an LRAD is both louder and more directionally focused so that the increased noise will be uncomfortably loud for those on the right-of-way while others remain unaffected. The LRAD is supposed to create a situation which is so uncomfortable that individuals would leave the right-of-way. However, there are other concerns with the use of such technology.

First, an LRAD can cause ear pain, vomiting, and migraines, which raises ethical issues. Secondly, an LRAD can cause a loss of equilibrium in some cases, which may make it more difficult for individuals to leave the right-of-way (Lewer & Davison, 2005).

Lastly, this technology has never been tested in the railroad environment so it remains unclear where such a device would be mounted, how it might be activated, and how effective it would be.

- **Current Use**
  The LRAD technology is not currently used by railroads, however, it has been proposed for use[45].
- **Evidence of Effectiveness for Rail**
  This technology is not being used within the railroad environment, thus there is no evidence for or against the effectiveness of this technology to mitigate suicide or trespass behaviors.
- **Evidence of Effectiveness for Other Means**
  This technology has never been considered for use to prevent or mitigate suicide by other means.
- **Evidence of Impact on Other Individuals**
  Long Range Acoustic Devices (LRAD) are not specifically targeted at suicide attempts. Though the technology has never been implemented in the railroad environment to mitigate trespass or suicide, LRAD has been used by the US military and was acquired by the New York State Police (NYSP) in 2004, as well as by several other police forces around the country including in Boston, San Diego, and Pittsburgh, for use as a non-lethal crowd control device[46]. However, concerns

were voiced over the potential use of this technology by the NYSP due to possible legal, policy, and human rights issues associated with it. The San Diego Police Department released a document detailing their acquisition of an LRAD device that mentioned potential concerns (including the possibility of hearing damage if operated too close)[47].

- **Feasibility of Railroad Implementation**
  Passenger Railroad Feasibility: In a railroad setting, it is assumed that an LRAD will make an individual attempting suicide uncomfortable to the point that they voluntarily remove themselves from the environment. To the knowledge of the authors, this belief currently has no scientific support. LRAD and similar technologies are intended to incapacitate an individual, which may result in the opposite effect that the railroad industry is attempting to achieve in this setting (i.e., the technology may make it more difficult for the trespasser to think or move out of the way). If a railroad is planning to implement LRAD or a similar technology, they must ensure that individuals can exit the right-of-way under their own power. They must also carefully consider all legal and human rights issues involved both for the trespasser as well as nearby passengers who may be affected, intentionally or otherwise, by the use of the technology. Other technologies which attempt to force the trespasser to exit the right-of-way by reducing comfort levels will encounter the same issues. Additionally, even though LRAD technology uses channelized sound and it should not greatly increase noise levels in adjacent areas, potential impacts on surrounding areas and the train crew/passengers must also be considered. Individuals living near the right-of-way, individuals in the train, and wildlife may be impacted by the addition of loud sounds.
  Freight Railroad Feasibility: Both freight and passenger operations will deal with similar challenges if they decide to implement LRAD, and both types of operations need to undergo much consideration about the impacts, both intended and unintended, before any testing is attempted.

Summary Table. Long Range Acoustic Devices (LRAD)

Target Population	Benefits	Known Issues	Summary
Individuals on right-of-way as the train approaches	• None of been shown	• Impact on suicides not known • May impair trespassers to a point where exiting the right- of-way is made difficult • Human rights concerns	Using Long Range Acoustic Devices (LRAD) on trespassers who are on the right-of-way as the train approaches. It has been postulated that using LRAD on trespassers may create such an unpleasant environment that the individual will leave the right-of-way voluntarily. There is no evidence that this countermeasure will accomplish this goal. In fact there is some evidence that the use of LRAD could hinder the individual's ability to successfully exit the right-of-way.

3.4.3. Speed Restrictions

When an individual has entered the railroad right-of-way, one way to avoid a collision is to stop the train before it strikes the individual. However, a train can take a significant distance to stop even after emergency braking has occurred. A freight train travelling at 100 km/hr (62 mi/hr) requires approximately 2 km (1.2 miles) to stop, while a passenger train travelling at 160 km/hr (100 mi/hr) requires a similar stopping distance[48]. A major factor affecting the braking distance of a train is its speed, especially for lighter non-freight trains, which have less force driving the train forward. While there are other influences on braking distance, such as the mass of the train or the gradient of the track, speed is one of the few factors that can be actively controlled by the train engineer. Reducing a train's speed will, to some degree, reduce its braking distance; however, the small reduction in braking distance may not be enough to prevent injury, especially on the open track, nor would it be justified in terms of the delays in freight and passenger traffic that reductions in speed will cause. Speed restrictions may also fall under Section

3.5. Reduction in Lethality of Train-Person Collision, however, the ideal goal of the technologies in this section would be to avoid a collision.

- **Current Use**
  Anecdotal evidence indicates that speed restrictions have been used in targeted areas as a means of preparing to avoid a potential train-person collision.[49] At least one commuter railroad system in the US has indicated that they communicate with local authorities or a station attendant if there is an individual at or near a station exhibiting suspicious behavior.[50] In these cases they will contact train drivers to slow the train when entering that station.
- **Evidence of Effectiveness for Rail**
  It has been suggested that reducing train speeds may be an effective way to reduce the likelihood of a collision if an individual enters the right-of-way. However, bringing a train to a complete stop is not an easy or quick task and is not guaranteed to avoid a collision. In the UK, the Rail Group Standard GM/RT 2042 (1996) established maximum braking distances for railway cars under their own braking power. This report found that the braking distance for a rail car traveling 55 mph must not exceed 2,953 feet, while the braking distance for a rail car traveling 20 mph must not exceed 640 feet. Though the braking distance reported in GM/RT 2042 was significantly reduced by the reduction in speed, the braking distances were still very large for relatively low speeds (20 mph). These speeds assume a single rail car with its own braking power; adding additional rail cars will increase the braking distance of the train. Additional factors, such as size, weight, grade, and traction will also have a substantial effect on the actual breaking distance. Berger and Mohan (1996) claim that, as with automobiles, the impact of the unprotected body with a train exceeding about 30 km/hr (19mph) or even lower is likely to be fatal. This calls into question how effective speed restrictions may be for reducing fatalities. Additionally, the US is currently focusing on expanding its use of high-speed rail, so implementing countermeasures that reduce train speeds are counter to the goals of increasing train speeds.
- **Evidence of Effectiveness for Other Means**
  The effect of speed restrictions on other means of suicide are not well known because the railroad is one of the few transportation-related suicide methods. However, there has been research into the effects of

speed restrictions on roadway fatalities. When speed limits were lowered to 20 mph from 30 mph in the UK, child pedestrian and child cyclist accidents were reduced by 67 percent (Pilkington, 2000). Still, train braking is very different from vehicle braking, so this evidence may not transfer directly to the railroad environment.

- **Evidence of Impact on Other Individuals**
  A reduction in speed, if effective, will affect both trespassers and those attempting suicide. If an individual who is attempting suicide remains on the right-of-way (i.e., they do not reconsider their action and remove themselves from the track voluntarily), reducing the train's speed will provide more time for the train to stop prior to the collision. However, if the individual on the right-of-way is a trespasser who does not wish to be struck by the train, then the reduced speed may provide additional time for the individual to exit the right-of-way safely. Therefore, the reduction in train speed may have a larger impact on non-intentional deaths than on suicides because the slower speeds provide two possible methods for avoiding collisions, while the train must fully stop for suicides.
- **Feasibility of Railroad Implementation**
  Passenger Railroad Feasibility: Reducing the speed of passenger trains is unlikely to have a dramatic effect on the number of suicide related fatalities on the railroad right-of-way. Passenger trains are lighter than freight trains, so a reduction in speed will have a more noticeable effect on the stopping distance of the train. Still, more research is needed to understand the effect of train speed on braking distance and the lethality of collisions at different train speeds.
  Freight Railroad Feasibility: Speed restrictions may be less effective for freight railroads due to the weight of freight trains when compared with passenger trains. The immense weight of some freight trains may require a large stopping distance even when the trains are moving at slow speeds, so the impact of the reduction in speed may be less.

3.4.4. Track Surveillance

One proposed countermeasure is to identify suspicious individuals prior to the arrival of the train by monitoring the railroad right-of-way. This countermeasure will not affect individuals who enter the right-of-way immediately prior to the arrival of the train, however, it may be able to identify individuals loitering on or near the right-of-way.

If an individual exhibiting suspicious behavior is identified, then the authorities or train crews can be alerted. The monitoring may be done with technology such as cameras or sensors (e.g., see the laser beam sensors in Figure 14), or direct monitoring of the right-of-way by a railroad employee or law enforcement official.

The steps that are taken after a suspicious individual is identified play a crucial role in this countermeasure's effectiveness.

Summary Table. Speed Restrictions

Target Population	Benefits	Known Issues	Summary
Individuals on right-of-way as the train approaches	• May affect both trespass and suicides	• Trains may not be able to stop despite the restrictions, especially heavier trains • Slower train strikes can still be fatal • Delayed delivery of passengers and freight	Reduce the train speed in targeted areas so that drivers have a better chance to stop if there is an individual on the right-of-way. Limiting train speeds may help a driver to brake more quickly, but in many instances the distance required to stop a train may still be too great to stop before a collision occurs (especially for heavier freight operations). Additionally, a slow moving train may still kill an individual if he or she is struck. The costs of delays in passenger and freight deliveries must be considered as well. Speed restrictions targeted at specific timeframes and locations may be effective, but need further analysis.

Figure 14. Track Surveillance with Laser Beam in UK.[51]

- **Current Use**
  Track surveillance is being used to detect trespassers in a limited capacity. A surveillance system on a railroad bridge in Pittsford, NY was tested from August 2011 through August 2004 (daSilva, Barron, & Carroll, 2012).The bridge was monitored using infrared and motion sensitive cameras. Once a trespasser was identified a local security attendant was notified and an alarm was triggered. After confirming that a trespasser was present, the security attendant would warn the trespasser, via bridge mounted loudspeakers, that they were trespassing on private property. Similar systems have been proposed for future use. In September 2013, a field research program was announced to test track surveillance technologies in the state of Maine.[52] This research effort is a collaboration between FRA, Maine Department of Transportation (DOT), the City of Brunswick, ME, and the Northern New England Passenger Railroad Authority (NNEPRA), among others. Remote presence detectors and wireless cameras (the details of which are not currently disclosed) will detect trespassers on the railroad right-of-way and alert the Brunswick Police, who will take appropriate action. Figure 14 shows an implementation of a track surveillance device currently being used in the UK at a grade crossing. Certain engineering firms have proposed the development of an obstruction sensor which is capable of detecting the presence of cars, trucks, and people on the right-of- way (Ignition Magazine, 2004). This technology proposes to use a strobe light to warn the train

engineer of the obstruction once one has been detected. Additional types of track surveillance, including microwave technology, are also being examined (Blacketer, Zaworski, and Hunter-Zaworski, 2005).

- **Evidence of Effectiveness for Rail**

  To date, the only trespasser detection system in the United States that has been evaluated was at a bridge in Pittsford, New York (NY) (daSilva, Barron, & Carroll, 2012). The results of the study were mixed. The surveillance system was able to identify a large number of trespassers and the system may have saved at least five lives in three separate incidents. However, the false alarm rate of the system was very high, with nearly double the amount of false alarms as positive detections.

  While no other studies have focused on surveillance systems in the railroad environment, there are studies that have investigated how certain technologies can detect intrusions on the railroad right-of-way. In 2005, two intrusion detection technologies designed for high-speed railroad crossings (a video based detection system and a microwave detection system) were field tested (Blacketer, Zaworski, & Hunter-Zaworski, 2005). Both systems were able to detect objects as small as eight inches, so detecting a person on the right-of-way is feasible. However, such systems have limitations. For example, directly monitoring the entire United States right-of-way at the same time is not possible, so trespassers may still be able to find regions of track that are unmonitored. Additionally, the steps that will be taken after a trespasser has been detected remain unclear and must be established.

  This type of countermeasure will require a plan that describes how the information about the trespasser is delivered, to whom it is delivered, and how suspicious behavior will be dealt with once it is identified. It is not enough to simply identify individuals who may be exhibiting behavior associated with a risk of suicide, one must act to intervene or to alert train drivers. The plan developed in Pittsford, NY is only one approach to dealing with detected trespassers and their plan may not work in all settings. For example, the bridge used in the NY evaluation is a very specific and limited region of track with clear locations where speakers could be mounted. If the surveillance technology is looking at broader regions, making announcements to trespassers with speakers may not be possible.

- **Evidence of Effectiveness for Other Means**
  Surveillance has been discussed in terms of suicides on bridges; however, no known empirical studies have tested its effectiveness in reducing suicide incidents (e.g., as discussed in the review of bridge jumping prevention by Gunnell, Nowers, and Bennewith, 2005). One news report stated that active monitoring of the Golden Gate Bridge by the Golden Gate Bridge Patrol, a suicide prevention program started in 1996, resulted in a reduction in suicide rates, with a reported 34 potential jumpers being stopped in the first nine months of the program[53]. Though 24 fatal jumps occurred during that time span, the numbers may have been higher were it not for the Patrol. Another news report claimed that while 33 suicides occurred on the Golden Gate Bridge in 2012, another 86 potential suicide attempts were successfully prevented by patrols on the bridge[54]. However, these reported cases of suicide prevention have not been studied to determine how effective these patrols have been. Additionally, a bridge has dedicated endpoints which provide specific locations that can be monitored as opposed to the right-of-way (or even hotspots on the right-of-way) which is much more open. This expansive open track does not provide the same finite location that a bridge does, making selecting surveillance locations more difficult.
- **Evidence of Impact on Other Individuals**
  Track surveillance may help prevent both suicide and trespass incidents. Right-of-way monitors, whether they rely on technology or active monitoring by individuals, will not initially differentiate between a trespasser intent on suicide and a trespasser who has other reasons. The care provided to the individual may differ depending on the trespasser's stated motivations, but the initial identification of individuals at-risk will rely solely on their presence on the right-of-way.
- **Feasibility of Railroad Implementation**
  Passenger Railroad Feasibility: Monitoring the right-of-way may allow train engineers or law enforcement officials to be warned of suspicious behavior on the right-of-way. However, if this plan is going to be effective, a process must be in place that manages the situation once an intrusion is detected. If the locomotive engineer is alerted, the impact of slowing the train must be considered. If law enforcement officials are notified via the surveillance system, they must have a plan in place to coordinate their efforts with the train

crews and respond to the scene quickly. Finally, this countermeasure will not have an effect on individuals who enter the right-of-way immediately before impact.

Freight Railroad Feasibility: The feasibility of track surveillance for freight and passenger operations will have similar benefits and challenges.

3.5. Reduction in Lethality of Train-Person Collision

Once an individual has been struck by a train, the only remaining barrier to death by suicide is preventing the strike from being lethal. The next type of countermeasure discussed is the reduction in the lethality of a train-person collision, as shown in Figure 15.

Summary Table. Track Surveillance

Target Population	Benefits	Known Issues	Summary
Individuals trespassing on rights-of-way	• May impact both trespass and suicide	• Requires constant surveillance • False alarms from animals and debris • Must have specific plan for intervention and/or enforcement	Monitoring the right-of-way (or sections of track) to identify individuals trespassing on or loitering near the right-of-way. Track surveillance may allow railroads to identify individuals who are trespassing. However, if this countermeasure is going to be effective at reducing suicides the railroads and/or law enforcement must be committed to dealing with individuals once they are identified.

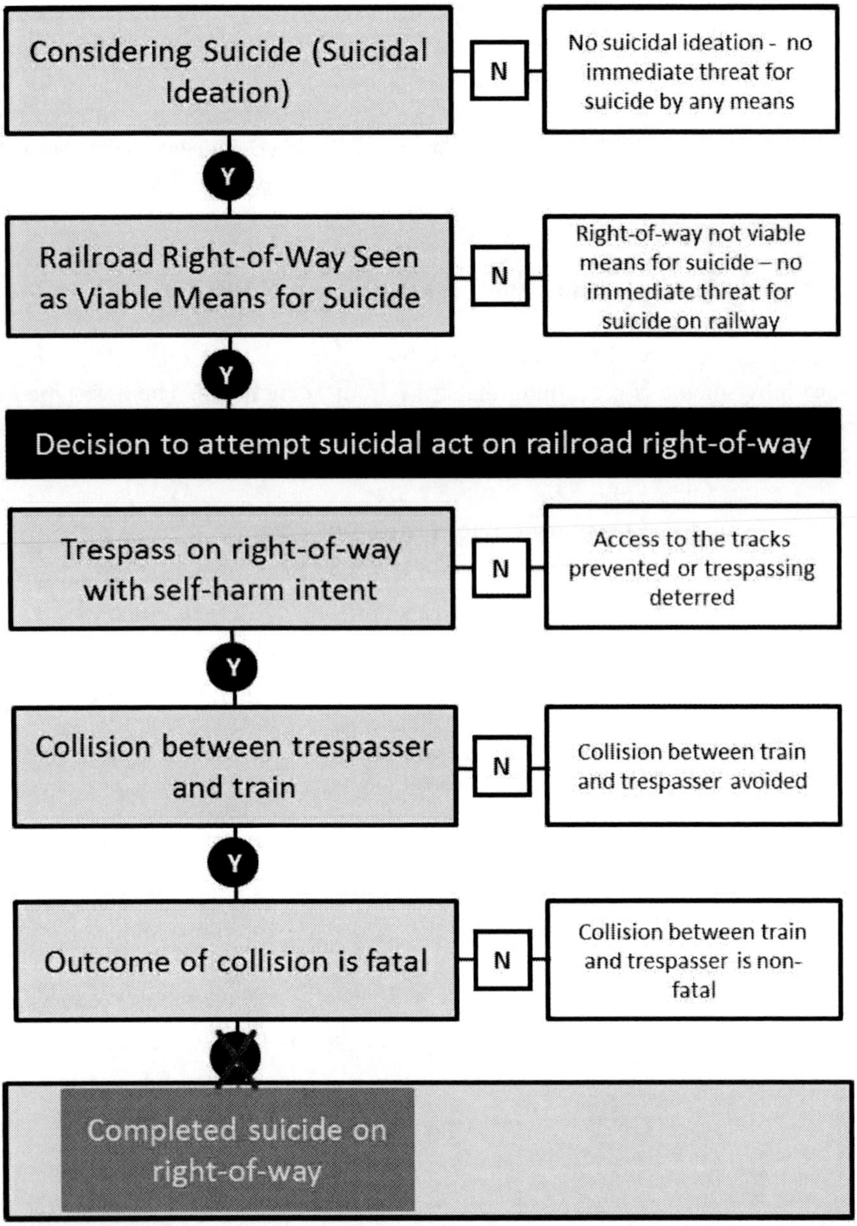

Figure 15. Countermeasures to Reduce the Lethality of a Train-Person Collision.

If a countermeasure reduces the lethality of a collision between a train and person, it assumes that a collision occurs (i.e., the collision can no longer be avoided). Once a collision is imminent, there are very few countermeasures which could reduce the possibility of a fatality. One such countermeasure with the potential to reduce the lethality of a strike is modifying the train itself. Various concepts and patents have been developed with this specific goal in mind; however, none have been produced for use so their potential for success is unknown.

3.5.1. Train Modification

It is been proposed that modifying the front of a train could make a train strike less lethal to a pedestrian. No specific modification has been tested or proven to be effective, but proposals include a modification to the lead unit of the train that would deflect the trespasser to the side of the right-of-way. These concepts are probably inspired by the *pilot*, or *cowcatcher*, that is often mounted on the front of a train. A pilot is a device that is used to deflect obstacles from the track, similar in both design and concept to a snow plow on the front of a truck defecting snow off of the road surface.

At least two patents exist which modify the front of a train with the goal of reducing the severity of a collision, though both focus more on collisions with land vehicles: US Patent #6293205 ("Train collision system") uses a flatbed rail car coupled to the front of the train with a ramp that leads to several deformable barrels (top of Figure 16); and US Patent #6474489 ("Collision Attenuator") which uses an energy absorbing assembly and a selectively-inflatable, externally mounted air bag to reduce the severity of a collision with a pedestrian or vehicle (bottom of Figure 16).

Several other similar patents have been developed for exterior airbags for motor vehicles to reduce the severity of collisions (e.g., US Patent #5732785, US Patent #7232001).

- **Current Use**
  Currently, there are no known train modifications in use for the purpose of reducing the lethality of a train-person collision.
- **Evidence of Effectiveness for Rail**
  To date, there have not been any tests to determine if such technologies would be effective or that they could be implemented in a railroad environment, nor whether the adoption of such changes would adversely affect the safety, efficiency or reliability of rail equipment, fixed infrastructure or operations.

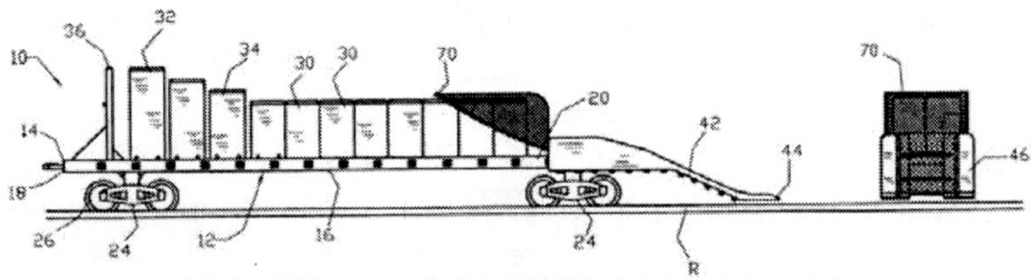

Train Collision System (US 6293205 B1): Paul A. Butler, 2001

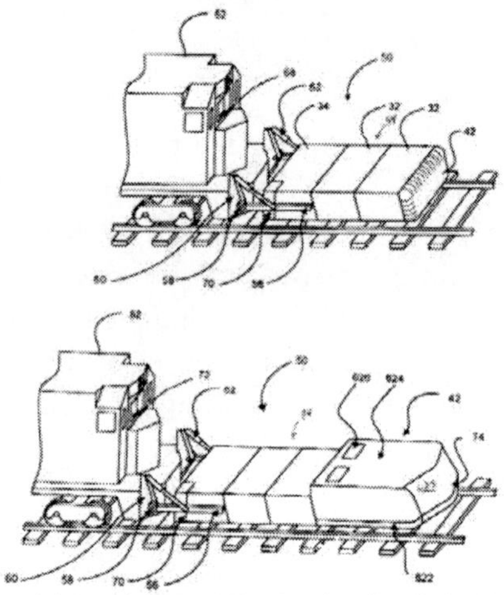

Collision Attenuator (US 6474489 B2): Thomas S. Payne and James M. Payne, 2002

Figure 16. Images from Two Patent Applications for Train Modification Systems.

- **Evidence of Effectiveness for Other Means**
  Similar countermeasures have not been implemented for other means of suicide. The railroad is the primary method of transportation-related suicide, so it is difficult to find other examples where other types of transportation are modified to mitigate suicide.
- **Evidence of Impact on Other Individuals**
  If a modification to the front of a train is effective at reducing the fatality of a train-person collision without impeding transportation or introducing additional operational hazards,, it would still come into contact with the individual. The effectiveness of this countermeasure will not differ regardless of the motivations or intent of the individual on the right-of-way. The patents described in this section are not specifically designed for suicides, but rather for any individual on the right-of-way. As mentioned above, patents have been developed for

exterior airbags for motor vehicles; however, none of these technologies have been tested for effectiveness in real world scenarios. However, reducing fatalities and severe injury is very different for trains and motor vehicles due to drastically different design characteristics and size (among other factors). In most motor vehicle accidents the pedestrian is first struck in the leg by the bumper of the vehicle, which provides time for external airbags to be deployed and protect the head. These challenges, in addition to massive differences in the force of the impact, may make translating similar safety enhancements to the railroad environment impractical.

- **Feasibility of Railroad Implementation**
  Passenger Railroad Feasibility: To date, modifying the front of a locomotive to reduce the lethality of a train-person collision has not been studied. No specific train modifications have been tested, so the actual cost or feasibility of implementation is unknown. Additionally, since such modifications have been proposed but not studied in the field, the effectiveness of any implementation is also unknown. Regulators and railroads will need to consider the impacts of any changes to the motive power needed to safely clear wayside structures (i.e. passenger rail platforms, signal system housings, etc.) or changes to the ability of maintenance crews to access parts located on the front of the locomotive, among numerous other considerations. There is no evidence that modifying the front of a locomotive will be an effective strategy and, at a minimum, a cost benefit analysis of such a modification must be carefully studied prior to any real-world implementation.
  Freight Railroad Feasibility: Train modification-related issues for passenger operations (as stated above) will also impact freight operations. However, the increased weight of freight trains, relative to passenger trains, may increase the severity of train-person impacts, which would make successful modifications even more difficult.

3.6. Improvement in Data Collection

In order to better understand where and why suicides occur on the railroad right-of-way, it is vital to collect accurate and consistent data on the incidents that occur. Without accurate data collection, it will not be possible to evaluate the impact of countermeasures against suicides. By improving the quality of the data being collected, one can more confidently assess the rates of both intentional (suicides) and unintentional (trespasser) fatalities on the railroad right-of-way. These potential mitigation strategies will not have an effect on suicides directly but may provide railroads with more meaningful data, which would allow the railroads to better determine which countermeasure may be most effective for their particular situation.

Better quality data will not only help railroads to understand the types of incidents occurring on their rights-of-way, but also to make comparisons across states or even countries. There are often discrepancies in reported rates of suicide. For example, Reynders, Scheerder, & Van Audenhove (2010) stated that the European Railway Agency recorded significantly higher rates of suicide than did the European Mortality Database (MDB), registering 34 percent more suicides and 9 percent more railway fatalities than the national statistics reported for Italy and France. Such discrepancies appear to be the norm rather than the exception.

Summary Table. Train Modification

Target Population	Benefits	Known Issues	Summary
Individuals who collide with a train -	• Reduce fatalities of those not dissuaded by other countermeasures	• High cost • Strike may be lethal despite modification • Unclear how odification would be deployed (if necessary)	Modifying the front of the train to bounce trespassers and those attempting suicide off to the side of the right-of-way without causing fatal injury. There is no evidence to date that a modification can be made to the front of a train that would successfully reduce the fatality of a train-person collision. Additionally the cost of implementing such a countermeasure on a large number of trains would likely be very high.

With a better understanding of each and every event (intentional and unintentional), more can be learned about preventing similar incidents. The strategy discussed in this section focuses on efforts that can be made after an incident has occurred. Specifically, Section 3.6.1 discusses how coroners and medical examiners should be trained to determine whether fatalities on the railroad rights-of-way are suicides or accidental.

Note that the subsection discussed below is slightly modified from those in the above sections on countermeasures. These changes were made because these strategies are not aimed to directly mitigate suicides on the right-of-way, but are instead aimed to improve data collection practices.

3.6.1. Training Coroners/Medical Examiners or Others to More Consistently Determine Suicidal Intent

Depending on the state in which the incident occurred, either a coroner or a medical examiner is responsible for determining the cause of death in the United States. While the cause of the death in a train collision may be blunt force trauma, the coroner or medical examiner must determine if the death was due to an intentional act (i.e., suicide) and record their determination on the death certificate. Medical examiners hold a medical degree and have been appointed by a state or local government. Many counties also require the medical examiner to be trained in forensic pathology. Coroners are elected positions, the qualifications for which are set by individual states, and in some cases by counties within the state.

With such a wide range in training and knowledge, the criteria used by coroners and examiners to determine if a railway fatality is accidental or intentional are probably inconsistent. These inconsistencies likely complicate comparisons between the rates of intentional and unintentional fatalities across the country, and they also may make it more difficult to measure the effectiveness of any countermeasure implementations. Without a true understanding of the relative number of suicides and trespasser incidents, it will not be possible to track how these rates change after a countermeasure has been implemented.

- **Current Knowledge**

  The death investigator is responsible for determining if a fatality was due to an act of suicide. He or she, depending on the jurisdiction (which can vary by county) is either a medical examiner or a coroner. As of 2011, 28 states used a coroner system or a mix of coroner and medical examiner systems (Davis, 2011). In Texas, justices of the peace may also perform coroner duties. Though documents exist to train individuals on the determination of death (e.g., the Center for Disease Control (CDC) *Medical Examiners' and Coroners' Handbook on Death Registration and Fetal Death Reporting,* 2003) it is unclear if such documents are used or followed during investigations. Currently, there are no known references to assist in the determination of suicide for fatalities on the railroad rights-of-way.

- **Evidence of Potential Impact for Rail**

  To date, there have been no investigations to discover if training medical examiners or coroners in determining the cause of death for incidents that occur on the railroad rights-of- way will impact the quality of data reporting. Though better consistency in the determinations of death between coroners and medical examiners will result in an improvement in the reliability of data being collected, it remains unclear if training will increase the accuracy of these determinations.

  Instead, it may be advantageous for the railroads or government to conduct their own, independent investigations for internal record keeping. In the UK a set of criteria, known as the Ovenstone Criteria, are used to classify all fatalities on the railroad right-of-way as suspected suicides or unintentional trespassers, and it contains criteria which, if met, should indicate a potential suicide (see Appendix C for full criteria). The Criteria states that presence of any of the following can be treated as sufficient evidence of a suspected suicide: suicide note, clear statement of suicidal intent to an informant, behavior demonstrates suicidal intent, previous suicide attempts, prolonged depression, and emotional instability. It may be possible for other railroads around the world to implement similar (though not identical) criteria, which would provide consistency for international communities' understanding of this problem.

- **Evidence of Impacts for Other Means**

  Guidelines for how to conduct a thorough investigation of the means of death are available, but not regulated. For example, the CDC revised their *Medical Examiners' and Coroners' Handbook on Death Registration and Fetal Death Reporting* in 2003. In this document, the CDC defines a suicide as a death which "results from an injury or poisoning as a result of an intentional, self-inflicted act committed to do self-harm or cause the death of one's self". Additionally, this report includes a list of evidence (explicit and/or implicit) which can be used to determine if the decedent fully understood the consequences of their actions (See Appendix D). Ensuring that all coroners and medical examiners are following the same guidelines may help standardize how determinations of suicide are made in the US.

- **Feasibility of Railroad Implementation**
  Passenger Railroad Feasibility: Educating medical examiners, coroners, and government staff could provide new insights into both unintentional and intentional trespassing fatalities.
  The ability to develop countermeasures and evaluate their effectiveness depends on the quality of the data being collected. The railroad's role in advancing this goal is less clear. One possibility is to adopt criteria that are similar to the Ovenstone in the United States. This would allow the railroads or the FRA to determine of the cause of death on their own. These Ovenstone determinations would not have any bearing on the coroner or medical examiner ruling, but would provide an objective tool for railroads to quickly and accurately determine the possible cause of death. This may help to improve data quality and speed up the rate that determinations are made.
  Freight Railroad Feasibility: The feasibility of educating coroners or medical examiners will have similar benefits and challenges for both freight and passenger operations.

4. CONCLUSION

Suicides on railroad rights-of-way not only affect the individual involved and their friends and family, but also those railroad personnel involved in or directly impacted by the incident. Railroads have begun to implement countermeasures which may reduce the number of suicides, including fencing and, on some passenger lines, posting signs that direct at-risk individuals to call a mental health crisis center hotline. It is increasingly important for railroad carriers to assess these countermeasures in terms of their effectiveness, especially given liability considerations, budgetary constraints and increased demands for railroad efficiency

Summary Table. Training Coroners/Medical Examiners or Others to More Consistently Determine Suicidal Intent

Target Population	Benefits	Known Issues	Summary
No target population. Goal is to improve data quality.	• Better data quality • Faster determination of cause of death • Better ability to track where and why incidents occurred • Better ability to assess countermeasur e effectiveness	• Different standards in each state • No current standards exist	Improving the ability of coroners or medical examiners to accurately determine the cause of railway deaths. Alternatively, identifying a means for railroad carriers to determine cause of death independently of other more official determinations. With better accuracy in the reporting of railroad fatalities, the railroads, FRA, and researchers can better understand the problem. Any efforts to improve the quality of the data being collected will help to determine what can be done to mitigate future incidents.

An individual who attempts suicide on the railroad right-of-way has a different motivation than a trespasser, who willfully disregards laws governing private property and had no intention of being struck, but either is oblivious to a train's presence or misjudged its speed, direction or velocity. On the other hand, an individual attempting suicide intends to be struck and killed by the train. In order for a suicide to occur on the right-of-way, the individual must enter the right-of-way, be struck by train or other pieces of on-track equipment, and suffer a strike that is severe enough to be fatal. For any of these actions to occur, the individual must view the railroad right- of-way as a viable means to achieve this self-harm. Each point in the process provides a location or time for a countermeasure to be implemented. The best method for preventing a suicide on the railroad right-of-way is to implement a variety of countermeasures aimed to mitigate suicide in different ways.

Initial countermeasures may focus on preventing the individual from deciding to attempt suicide or reducing the attractiveness of the right-of-way as a viable means for suicide. These countermeasures are designed to influence individuals on a psychological level and change the way they think about suicide or the railroad through public awareness, or providing contact information for people who are able to help the at –risk individual. If attempts to deter these individuals psychologically are not effective (either because the message did not reach them or the message was ineffective) then the next series of countermeasures are aimed at physically preventing suicides from occurring on the right-of-way. These countermeasures attempt to prevent access to the right-of-way, avoid the impact, or lessen its severity. Lastly, in order to understand the effects that each of these countermeasures are having, one must be able to confidently measure how frequently suicides or suicide attempts occur. Collecting and maintaining better, more accurate and reliable data is vital to advancing our understanding of suicides on railroad rights-of-way and discerning how or if countermeasure efforts are influencing suicide occurrences.

Not all of the countermeasures discussed will be feasible for railroads to implement. For example, a freight railroad cannot implement gatekeeper training, platform edge doors, or anti- suicide pits. Also, many of these countermeasures remain untested and, if implemented without careful evaluation, may cause unintended consequences or result in costs without positive returns on the investment. Railroads should consider which combinations of countermeasures will affect the types of incidents they wish to prevent. Railroads may also consider reaching out to other potential stakeholders, such as local communities or land owners, to collaborate in implementing or maintaining countermeasures. For example, if a passenger railway line has been the location of suicides near a school, then perhaps partnerships with school counselors, targeted public awareness in collaboration with the local community, or a carefully worded signage campaign may be most effective.

Additionally, suicides on the railroad right-of-way are not only an issue of concern for the railroad company, but also for the community in which these incidents are occurring. Railroads may consider collaborating with local communities in areas where multiple incidents have occurred and coordinate resources to implement successful countermeasures. Many of the countermeasures discussed in this document can be implemented in targeted areas where they are most needed. This will likely to be the cases when a community partnership will be most effective. For example, a community may be willing to help fund the installation or maintenance of a fence in an area that is known to be susceptible to suicide attempts. A partnership where both parties help to defray the full cost of such countermeasures is likely to help both the railroad and the community in the long run.

5. References

Ahmedani, B. K., Simon, G. E., Stewart, C., Beck, A., Waitzfelder, B. E., Rossom, R., Lynch, F., Owen-Smith, A., Hunkeker, E. M., Whiteside, U., Operskalski, B. H., Coffey, M. J. & Solberg, L. I. (2014). Health care contacts in the year before suicide death. *Journal of General Internal Medicine*, 1-8.

Andriessen, K. & Krysinska, K. (2012). Railway suicide in Belgium 1998–2009: Incidence and prevention. Crisis: *The Journal of Crisis Intervention and Suicide Prevention*, *33*(1), 39.

Anonymous (2009, November 4). Japan installs 'anti-suicide blue lights' at railway platforms, *Metro.* Retrieved from http:// www.metro.co.uk/ news/ world/762337-japan-installs-anti-suicide- blue-lights-at-railway-platforms.

Armstrong, T. & Costello, E. (2002). Community studies on adolescent substance use, abuse, or dependence and psychiatric comorbidity. *Journal of Consultation Clinical Psychology*, *70*, 1224-1239.

Aseltine, R. H. Jr. & DeMartino, R. (2004). An outcome evaluation of the SOS suicide prevention program. *American Journal of Public Health*, *94*(3), 446-451.

Barney, D., Haley, D. & Nidandros, G. (2001). *Calculating Train Braking Distance.* 6th Australian Workshop on Safety Critical Systems and Software, Brisbane, Australia.

Beautrais, A. L. (2001). Risk Factors for Suicide and Attempted Suicide Among Young People. *Australian and New Zealand of Psychiatry*, *3*(34), 420-436.

Berman, A., Sundararaman, R., Price, A., Marshall, K., Martino, M., Doucette, A., Chase, S. & Gabree, S. (2013). *Defining Characteristics of Intentional Fatalities on Railway Rights-of-Way in the United States*, 2007 – 2010. DOT/FRA/ORD-13/25.

Bennewith, O., Nowers, M. & Gunnell, D. (2007). Effect of barriers on the Clifton suspension bridge, England, on local patterns of suicide: implications for prevention. *The British Journal of Psychiatry*, *190*(3), 266-267.

Berger, L. R. & Mohan, D. (1996). *Injury control: a global view*. Oxford University Press, USA.

Blacketer, R., Zaworski, J. R. & Hunter-Zaworski, K. M. (2005). Field testing of intrusion detection technologies for high-speed rail crossings. *Transportation Research Record: Journal of the Transportation Research Board*, *1918*(1), 10-17.

Bohanna, I. & Wang, X. (2012). Media guidelines for responsible reporting of suicide: a review of effectiveness. *Crisis*, *33*(4), 190-198.

Brådvik, L. (2013). Last Suicide Attempt before Completed Suicide in Severe Depression: An Extended Suicidal Process May Be Found in Men Rather Than Women. *Archives of Suicide Research*, *17*(4), 426-433.

Brådvik, L. & Berglund, M. (2011). Repetition of suicide attempts across episodes of severe depression: behavioural sensitisation found in suicide group but not in controls. *BMC Psychiatry*, *11*(1), 5.

Butler, P. A. (2001). *U.S. Patent No. 6,293,205*. Washington, DC: U.S. Patent and Trademark Office.

Chen, Y. Y., Liao, S. F., Teng, P. R., Tsai, C. W., Fan, H. F., Lee, W. C. & Cheng, A. T. (2012). The impact of media reporting of the suicide of a singer on suicide rates in Taiwan. *Social Psychiatry and Psychiatric Epidemiology*, *47*(2), 215-221.

Christiansen, E. & Frank Jensen, B. (2007). Risk of repetition of suicide attempt, suicide or all deaths after an episode of attempted suicide: a register-based survival analysis. *Australasian Psychiatry*, *41*(3), 257-265.

Classen, C. A., Yip, P. S., Corcoran, P., Bossarte, R. M., Lawrence, B. A. & Currier, G. (2010) National suicide rates a century after Durkeheim: do we know enough to estimate error? *Suicide and Life Threatening Behaviour*, *40*, 193-223.

Coats, T. J. & Walter, D. P. (1999). Effect of station design on death in the London Underground: observational study. *BMJ: British Medical Journal*, *319*(7215), 957.

Cole, B. L. (2005). When is artificial light hazardous? *Clinical and Experimental Optometry: Journal of the Australian Optometrical Association*, *88*(4), 195-196.

Cooper, J., Kapur, N., Webb, R., Lawlor, M., Guthrie, E., Mackway-Jones, K. & Appleby, L. (2005). Suicide after deliberate self-harm: a 4-year cohort study. *American Journal of Psychiatry*, *162*, 297–303.

Coryell, W. H. (2013). Risk factors for suicide attempts and completions. In M. Keller & W.H. Coryell (Eds), *Clinical Guide to Depression and*

Bipolar Disorder: Findings From the Collaborative Depression Study (pp.71-80) Arlington, VA: American Psychiatric Publishing.

Crosby, A. E., Ortega, L. & Melanson, C. (2011). *Self Directed Violence Surveillance: Uniform Definitions and Recommended Data Elements*. Atlanta, GA: Centers for Disease Control & Prevention, National Center for Injury Prevention and Control.

Daniel, A. E. (2006). Preventing suicide in prison: a collaborative responsibility of administrative, custodial, and clinical staff. *Journal of the American Academy of Psychiatry and the Law Online*, *34*(2), 165-175.

DaSilva, M., Barron, W. & Carroll, A. (2012). *Highway Rail Grade Crossing Safety Research: Railroad Competition Infrastructure Trespassing Detection Systems Research in Pittsford, New York*. DOT-VNTSC-FRA-05-07.

Dankova, I. (2011). *The Sameness Around Us* (Unpublished Manuscript).

Davis, Gregory. (May 2011). *Medical Examiner and Coroner Systems*. Retrieved from http://emedicine.medscape.com/article/1785357-overview.

Dinkel, A., Baumert, J., Erazo, N. & Ladwig, K. H. (2011). Jumping, lying, wandering: Analysis of suicidal behaviour patterns in 1,004 suicidal acts on the German railway net. *Journal of Psychiatric Research*, *45*(1), 121-125.

Dumesnil, H. & Verger, P. (2009). Public awareness campaigns about depression and suicide: a review. *Psychiatric Services*, *60*(9), 1203-1213.

Editorial: The agenda - Development process of the United States national action alliance for suicide prevention research prioritization task force [Editorial]. (2013). *Crisis*, *34*(3), 147-155.

Etzersdorfer, E. & Sonneck, G. (1998). Preventing suicide by influencing mass-media reporting. The Viennese experience, 1980–1996. *Archives of Suicide Research*, *4*, 67–74.

Etzersdorfer, E., Sonneck, G. & Nagel-Kuess, S. (1992). Newspaper reports and suicide. *The New England Journal of Medicine*, *327*, 502-503.

Farmer, R., O'Donnell, I. A. N. & Tranah, T. (1991). Suicide on the London Underground system. *International Journal of Epidemiology*, *20*(3), 707-711.

George, B. F. (2008). *Rail Trespasser Fatalities: Developing Demographic Profiles*.

Gist, R. (2014) *Proposed Key Elements of Critical Incident Intervention Program for Reducing the Effects of Potentially Traumatic Exposure on Train Crews to Grade Crossing and Trespasser Incidents* – Not yet published.

Glatt, K. M. (1987). Helpline: suicide prevention at a suicide site. *Suicide and Life-Threatening Behavior*, *17*(4), 299-309.

Glickman G., Byrne, B., Pineda, C., Hauck, W. W. & Brainard G. C. (2006). Light therapy for seasonal affective disorder with blue narrow-band light-emitting diodes (LEDs). *Biological Psychiatry*, *59*, 502-507.

Goldsmith, S. K., Pellmer, T. C., Kleinman, A. M. & Bunney, W. E. (2002). *Reducing Suicide: A National Imperative*. Washington, DC: National Academies Press.

Goldston, D. B. (2004). Conceptual issues in understanding the relationship between suicidal behavior and substance use during adolescence. *Drug and Alcohol Dependence*, *7*(76), s79- s91.

Gosney, H. & Hawton, K. (2007). Inquest verdicts: youth suicides lost. *Psychiatric Bulletin*, *25*, 43-45.

Gould, M. S., Cross, W., Pisani, A. R., Munfakh, J. L. & Kleinman, M. (2013). Impact of applied suicide intervention skills training on the national suicide prevention lifeline. *Suicide and Life- Threatening Behaviour*, *43*(6), 676-691.

Gould, M. S., Kalafat, J., HarrisMunfakh, J. L. & Kleinman, M. (2007). An evaluation of crisis hotline outcomes part 2: suicidal callers. *Suicide and Life-Threatening Behavior*, *37*(3), 338-352.

Guggenheim, F. G. & Weisman, A. D. (1972). Suicide in the subway: publicly witnessed attempts of 50 cases. *The Journal of Nervous and Mental Disease*, *155*(6), 404-409.

Gunnell, D., Nowers, M. & Bennewith, O. (2005). Suicide by jumping: is prevention possible. *Suicidologi*, *10*(2), 15-17.

Hakki, S. & Hakki, A. H. (2007). U.S. Patent No. 7, 232,001. Washington, DC: *U.S. Patent and Trademark Office*.

Ham, W., Mueller, H., Ruffolo, J. J. & Guerry, K. (1980). The Nature of Retinal Radiation Damage: Dependence on Wavelength, Power Level and Exposure Time. *Vision Resolution*, *20*(12), 1105-1111.

Hawton, K. (2002). United Kingdom legislation on pack sizes of analgesics: background, rationale, and effects on suicide and deliberate self-harm. *Suicide and Life-Threatening Behavior*, *32*(3), 223-229.

Hor, K. & Taylor, M. (2010). Suicide and Schizophrenia: a systematic review of rates and risk factors. *Journal of Psychopharmacology*, *24*(4 supplement), 81-90.

Hubner-Liebermann, B., Neuner, T., Hegerl, U., Hajak, G., et al. (2010). Reducing suicides through an alliance against depression? *General Hospital Psychiatry*, *32*(5), 514-518.

Huh, G. Y., Jo, G. R., Kim, K. H., Ahn, Y. W. & Lee, S. Y. (2009). Imitative suicide by burning charcoal in the southeastern region of Korea: The influence of mass media reporting. *Legal Medicine, 11*, S563-S564.

Ichikawa, M., Inada, H. & Kumeji, M. (2013). Reconsidering the effects of blue-light installation for prevention of railway suicides. *Journal of Affective Disorders*, 152-154,183-184 DOI: http:// dx.doi.org/ 10.1016/ j.jad.2013.09.006.

Isaac, M., Elias, B., Katz, L. Y., Belik, S. L., Deane, F. P., Enns, M. W. & Sareen, J. (2009). Gatekeeper training as a preventative intervention for suicide: a systematic review. *Canadian Journal of Psychiatry, 54*(4), 260-268.

Jashinsky, J., Burton, S. H., Hanson, C. L., West, J., Giraud-Carrier, C., Barnes, M. D. & Argyle, T. (2014). Tracking suicide risk factors through Twitter in the US. *Crisis, 35*(1), 51-59.

Jáuregui, J., Martínez, M. L., Rubio, G. & Santo-Domingo, J. (1999). Patients who attempted suicide and failed to attend mental health centers. *European Psychiatry, 14*, 205–209.

Joiner, T. E. (2005). *Why people die by suicide*. Cambridge, MA: Harvard University Press. Kessler, R. C., Downey, G., Stipp, H., & Milavsky, J. R. (1989). Network television news stories about suicide and short-term changes in total US suicides. *The Journal of Nervous and Mental Disease, 177*(9), 551-555.

King, E. & Frost, N. (2005). The New Forest suicide prevention initiative (NFSPI). *Crisis: The Journal of Crisis Intervention and Suicide Prevention, 26*(1), 25-33.

Kunrath, S., Baumert, J. & Ladwig, K. H. (2011). Increasing railway suicide acts after media coverage of a fatal railway accident? An ecological study of 747 suicidal acts. *Journal of Epidemiology and Community Health, 65*(9), 825-828.

Ladwig, K. H., Kunrath, S., Lukaschek, K. & Baumert, J. (2012). The railway suicide death of a famous German football player: Impact on the subsequent frequency of railway suicide acts in Germany. *Journal of Affective Disorders, 136*(1), 194-198.

Lam, R.W., Tam, E.M., Shiah, I.S., Yatham, L.N. & Zis, A.P. (2000). Effects of Light Therapy on Suicidal Ideation in Patients with Winter Depression. *Journal of Clinical Psychiatry., 61*, 30-32

Law, C. K. & Yip, P. S. F. (2011). An economic evaluation of setting up physical barriers in railway stations for preventing railway injury:

evidence from Hong Kong. *Journal of Epidemiology and Community Health*, *65*(10), 915-920.

Leon, A. C., Keller, M. B., Fiedorowicz, J. G., Coryell, W. H. Endicott, J. & Keller, M. B. (2011). Antidepressants and risks of suicide and suicide attempts: a 27-year observational study, *Journal of Clinical Psychiatry*, *72*, 580-586.

Leon, A. C., Friedman, R. A., Sweeney, J. A., Brown, R. P. & Mann, J. J. (1990). Statistical issues in the identification of risk factors for suicidal behavior: the application of survival analysis. *Psychiatry Research*, *31*(1), 99-108.

Lewer, N. & Davison, N. (2005). Non-lethal technologies—an overview. *Disarmament Forum, 1*, 37-51.

Lindekilde, K. & Wang, A. G. (1985). Train suicide in the county of Fyn 1979–82. *Acta Psychiatrica Scandinavica*, *72*(2), 150-154.

Linsley, K. R., Schapira, K. & Kelly, T. P. (2001). Open verdict v. suicide—importance to research. *British Journal of Psychiatry*, *17*(8), 465-468.

Litman, R. E., Farberow, N. L., Shneidman, E. S., Heilig, S. M. & Kramer, J. A. (1965). Suicide-prevention telephone service. *JAMA: The Journal of the American Medical Association*, *192*(1), 21-25.

Lukaschek, K., Baumert, J. & Ladwig, K. H. (2011). Behaviour patterns preceding a railway suicide: Explorative study of German Federal Police officers' experiences. *BMC Public Health*, *11*(1), 620.

Luoma, J. B., Martin, C. E. & Pearson, J. L. (2002). Contact with Mental Health and Primary Care Providers Before Suicide: a Review of the Evidence. *American Journal of Psychiatry*, *159*(6), 909-916.

Martino, M., Chase, S. & Gabree, S. (2013). *Demographic Profile of Intentional Fatalities on Railroad Rights-of-Way in the United States*. FRA-RR-13-36.

Matsubayashi, T., Sawada, Y. & Ueda, M. (2013). Does the installation of blue lights on train platforms prevent suicide? A before-and-after observational study from Japan. *Journal of Affective Disorders*, *147*, 385-388.

Mishara, B. L. (1999). Conceptions of death and suicide in children ages 6–12 and their implications for suicide prevention. *Suicide and Life-Threatening Behavior*, *29*(2), 105-118.

Miret, M., Ayuso-Mateos, J. L., Sanchez-Moreno, J. & Vieta, E. (2013). Depressive disorders and suicide: Epidemiology, risk factors, and burden. (2013) *Neuroscience and Biobehavioural Reviews*, *37*, 2372-2374.

Niederkrotenthaler, T., Logan, J. E., Karch, D. L. & Crosby, A. (2014). Characteristics of US Suicide Decedents in 2005–2010 Who Had Received Mental Health Treatment. *Psychiatric Services*, *65*(3), 387-390.

Niederkrotenthaler, T., Voracek, M., Herberth, A., Till, B., Strauss, M., Etzersdorfer, E., Eisenwort, & Sonneck, G. (2010). Role of media reports in completed and prevented suicide: Werther v. Papageno effects. *The British Journal of Psychiatry*, *197*(3), 234-243.

Niederkrotenthaler, T., Till, B., Kapusta, N. D., Voracek, M., Dervic, K. & Sonneck, G. (2009). Copycat effects after media reports on suicide: A population-based ecologic study. *Social Science & Medicine*, *69*(7), 1085-1090.

Niederkrotenthaler, T., Herberth, A. & Sonneck, G. (2007). The "Werther-effect: legend or reality? *Neuropsychiatric*, *21*(4), 284-290.

Nordentoft, M. & Sogaard, M. (2005). Registration psychiatric evaluation and adherence to psychiatric treatment after suicide attempt. *Nordic Journal of Psychiatry*, *59*, 213–216.

O'Donnell, I. & Farmer, R. D. (1992). Suicidal acts on metro systems: an international perspective. *Acta Psychiatrica Scandinavica*, *86*, 60–63.

Oordt, M. S., Jobes, D. A., Fonseca V. P. & Schmidt, S. M. (2009). Training Mental Health Professionals to Assess and Manage Suicidal Behavior: Can Provider Confidence and Practice Behaviors Be Altered? *Suicide Life-Threatening Behavior*, *39*(1), 21-32.

Payne, T. S. & Payne, J. M. (2003). *U.S. Patent No. 6,619,491*. Washington, DC: U.S. Patent and Trademark Office.

Pearson, J. L., Stanley, B., King, C. A. & Fisher, C. B. (2001). Intervention research with persons at high risk for suicidality: Safety and ethical considerations. *The Journal of Clinical Psychiatry*, *62* (supplement 25), 17–26.

Phillips, D. P. (1974). The influence of suggestion on suicide: Substantive and theoretical implications of the Werther effect. *American Sociological Review*, *39*, 340-354.

Pilkington, P. (2000). Reducing the speed limit to 20 mph in urban areas: Child deaths and injuries would be decreased. *BMJ: British Medical Journal*, *320*(7243), 1160.

Praschak-Rieder, N., Neumeister, A., Hesselmann, B., Willeit, M., Barnas, C. & Kasper, S. (1997). Suicidal tendencies as a complication of light therapy for seasonal affective disorder: a report of three cases. *The Journal of Clinical Psychiatry*, *58*(9), 389-392.

Railroad Accidents/Incidents: Reports Classification and Investigations, 49 *C.F.R.* § 225. Ran, B., & Huang, W. (1998). *U.S. Patent No. 5,732,785.* Washington, DC: U.S. Patent and Trademark Office.

Ratnayake, R., Links, P. S. & Eynan, R. (2007). Suicidal behavior on subway systems: A review of the epidemiology. *Journal of Urban Health*, *84*(6), 766-781.

Reisch, T. & Michel, K. (2005). Securing a suicide hot spot: effects of a safety net at the Bern Muenster Terrace. *Suicide and Life-Threatening Behavior*, *35*(4), 460-467.

Reme, C. E., Wenzel, A., Grimm, G. & Iseli, H. P. (2003). Mechanisms of Blue Light-Induced Retinal Degeneration and the Potential Relevance for Age-Related Macular Degeneration and Inherited Retinal Diseases. *SLTBR Annual Meeting Abstracts 2003; Abstract 3.5 Chronobiology International*, *20*(6), 1186-1187

Requiring certain health professionals to complete education in suicide assessment, treatment, and management. House Bill 2366 – 2011-2012

Reynders, A., Scheerder, G. & Van Audenhove, C. (2011). The reliability of suicide rates: An analysis of railway suicides from two sources in fifteen European countries. *Journal of Affective Disorders*, *131*(1), 120-127.

Royal College of Psychiatrists, working group. (2010). *Self-Harm, Suicide and Risk: Helping People who Self Harm*. Retrieved from http:// www. rcpsych.ac.uk/files/pdfversion/cr158.pdf

Rutz, W., Knorring, L. V. & Wålinder, J. (1992). Long-term effects of an educational program for general practitioners given by the Swedish Committee for the Prevention and Treatment of Depression. *Acta Psychiatrica Scandinavica*, *85*(1), 83-88.

Ryan, B. (2013, March). Prevention Measures for Railway Suicide and Trespass- Do We Know What Works? UIC. Org. UIC electronic newsletter, Nr 336.

Seiden, R. H. (1978). Where Are They Now? A Follow-up Study of Suicide Attempters from the Golden Gate Bridge. *Suicide and Life-Threatening Behavior*, *8*(4), 203-216.

Signorini, A., Segre, A. M. & Polgreen, P. M. (2011). The use of Twitter to track levels of disease activity and public concern in the U.S. during the influenza A H1N1 pandemic. *PLoS One*, *6*(5), e19467.

Sisask, M. & Värnik, A. (2012). Media roles in suicide prevention: a systematic review. *International Journal of Environmental Research and Public Health*, *9*(1), 123-138.

Sonneck, G., Etzersdorfer, E. & Nagel-Kuess, S. (1994). Imitative suicide on the Viennese subway. *Social Science & Medicine*, *38*(3), 453-457.

Stack, S. (1990). Audience receptiveness, the media, and aged suicide, 1968–1980. *Journal of Aging Studies*, *4*(2), 195-209.

Stuart, C., Waalen PhD, J. K. & Haelstromm, E. (2003). Many helping hearts: An evaluation of peer gatekeeper training in suicide risk assessment. *Death studies*, *27*(4), 321-333.

Sudak, H. & Sudak, D. (2005). The Media and Suicide. *Academic Psychiatry*, 29(5), 495-499. Taghaddos, H. (2002). *U.S. Patent No. 6,375,251*. Washington, DC: U.S. Patent and Trademark Office.

Taylor, H. R., Munoz, B., West, S., Bressler, N. M., Bressler, S. B. & Rosenthal F. S. (1990). Visible Light and Risk Age Related Macular Degeneration. *Transactions of the American Ophthalmological Society*, *88*, 163-178.

Van Aalst, J. A., Shotts, S. D., Vitsky, J. L., Bass, S. M., Miller R. S., Meador, K. G. & Morris J. A. (1992). Long-term follow-up of unsuccessful violent suicide attempts: Risk factors for subsequent attempts. *Journal of Trauma*, *33*(3), 457-464.

Wang, A. G. & Mortensen, G. (2006). Core features of repeated suicidal behaviour. *Social Psychiatry and Psychiatric Epidemiology*, *41*(2), 103-107.

Watanabe, Y. (2011). A study on the effect of blue light illumination upon smoking behavior. *Jinbun Kenkyu: Studies in Humanities*, *175*, 161–175.

World Health Organization – Western Pacific Region. (2010). *Towards evidence-based suicide prevention programmes*. Geneva: WHO Press.

Wu, Jiangmei. (2004). *Blue light induced retinal damage* (Doctoral Dissertation, Karolinska Institutet).

Wyman, P. A., Brown, C. H., Inman, J., Cross, W., Schmeelk-Cone, K., Guo, J. & Pena, J. B. (2008). Randomized trial of a gatekeeper program for suicide prevention: 1-year impact on secondary school staff. *Journal of Consulting and Clinical Psychology*, *76*(1), 104.

van Houwelingen, C. A. & Kerkhof, A. J. (2008). Mental healthcare status and psychiatric diagnoses of train suicides. *Journal of Affective Disorders*, *107*(1), 281-284.

Yip, P. S., Fu, K. W., Yang, K. C., Ip, B. Y., Chan, C. L., Chen, E. Y. & Hawton, K. (2006). The effects of a celebrity suicide on suicide rates in Hong Kong. *Journal of Affective Disorders*, *93*(1), 245-252.

APPENDIX A. FRA GUIDE DEFINITIONS

Below are definitions from the FRA Guide for Preparing Accident/ Incident Reports (May 2011).

The following italicized text is from Section 2. Definitions: Classification of Persons:

Worker on Duty–Railroad Employee (Class A). *An individual who receives direct monetary compensation from the railroad. Whether the worker is under pay will generally, but not always, be the deciding factor for determining "on duty" status. An employee who is not under pay, but engaged in work-related activity is "on duty."*

Note: An employee in deadhead transportation is considered an "employee on duty," regardless of the mode of transportation. Deadhead transportation occurs when an employee is traveling at the direction or authorization of the carrier to or from an assignment, or the employee is involved with a means of conveyance furnished by the carrier or compensated for by the carrier.

Exception: If an employee is housed by the carrier in a facility such as a motel, and part of the service provided by the motel is the transportation of the employee to and from the work site, any reportable injury to the employee during such transit is to be recorded as that of a Railroad Employee Not On Duty (Class B). Likewise, if the employee decides upon other means of transportation that is not authorized or provided, and for which he would not have been compensated by the railroad, the injury is not considered work-related.

Railroad Employee Not On Duty (Class B). *An individual who receives direct monetary compensation from the railroad and who is on railroad property for purposes connected with his or her employment or with other railroad permission but is not "on duty."*

Worker on Duty–Contractor (Class F). *An employee of a contracting agency for a railroad who does not receive direct monetary compensation from the railroad and who, while on railroad property, is engaged in either 1) the operation of on-track equipment, or 2) any other safety- sensitive function for the railroad as defined in § 209.303. Section 209.303 describes "safety-sensitive functions" as applying to the following individuals:*

(a) Railroad employees who are assigned to perform service subject to the Hours of Service Act (45 U.S.C. 61-64b[55]) during a duty tour, whether or not the person has performed or is currently performing such service, and any person who performs such service;
(b) Railroad employees or agents who:
  (1) Inspect, install, repair, or maintain track and roadbed;
  (2) Inspect, repair, or maintain, locomotives, passenger cars, and freight cars;
  (3) Conduct training and testing of employees when the training or testing is required by the FRA's safety regulations; or
(c) Railroad managers, supervisors, or agents when they:
  (1) Perform the safety-sensitive functions listed in paragraphs (a) and (b) of this section;
  (2) Supervise and otherwise direct the performance of the safety-sensitive functions listed in paragraph (a) and (b) of this section; or
  (3) Are in a position to direct the commission of violations of any of the requirements of parts 213 through 236 of this title.

Note: There have been amendments and additions to the set of railroad safety regulations found in the CFR; thus, the term "safety-sensitive functions" in § 209.303(c)(3) is interpreted to include railroad managers, supervisors, etc., when they are in a position to direct the commission of violations of any of the requirements of Parts 213 through 240 of 49 CFR. Hours worked by persons in the Class F, G, H, and I categories are not reported on any FRA form.

Contractor–Other (Class G). *A contractor employee for a railroad who does not receive direct monetary compensation from the railroad and who is not engaged in either 1) the operation of on-track equipment, or 2) any other safety-sensitive function for the railroad. Hours worked by this person are not reported on any FRA form.*

Worker on Duty–Volunteer (Class H). *A volunteer who does not receive direct monetary compensation from the railroad and who is engaged in either 1) the operation of on-track equipment, or 2) any other safety-sensitive function for the railroad as defined in § 209.303. (See this list under "Worker on Duty–Contractor.") Hours worked by a "Worker on Duty–Volunteer" (Class H) are not reported on any FRA form.*

Volunteer–Other (Class I). *A volunteer who does not receive direct monetary compensation from the railroad and who is not engaged in either 1) the operation of on-track equipment, or 2) any other safety-sensitive function for the railroad as defined in § 209.303. Hours worked by this person also not reported on any FRA form.*

Passengers On Trains (Class C). *Persons who are on, boarding, or alighting railroad cars for the purpose of travel.*

Nontrespassers–On Railroad Property (Class D). *Persons lawfully on that part of railroad property that is used in railroad operation (other than those herein defined as employees, passengers, trespassers, volunteers, or contractor employees), and persons adjacent to railroad premises when they are injured as the result of the operation of a railroad. This class also includes other persons on vessels or buses, whose use arises from the operation of a railroad.*

Nontrespassers–Off Railroad Property (Class J). *An injury "off railroad property" includes an injury resulting from an event, such as a derailment or collision, that begins on railroad property but ends on public or private non-railroad property, so long as the injury is incurred while the person is physically located off railroad property. Similarly, if a derailment results in a release of hazardous materials onto public or private non-railroad property and the hazardous material injures a "Nontrespasser" located on public or private non-railroad property, the injury is reported as an injury to "Nontrespassers–Off Railroad Property" (Class J).*

Conversely, injuries to nontrespassers occurring while on public or private railroad property are reported as injuries to "Nontrespassers–On Railroad Property" (Class D).

Trespassers (Class E). *Persons who are on the part of railroad property used in railroad operation and whose presence is prohibited, forbidden, or unlawful. Employees who are trespassing on railroad property are to be reported as "Trespassers" (Class E).*

Note: A person on a highway-rail grade crossing should not be classified as a Trespasser (Class E) unless: 1) the crossing is protected by gates or other similar barriers, which were closed when the person went on the crossing, or 2) the person attempted to pass over, under, or between cars or locomotives of a consist occupying the crossing. A person or vehicle that enters the crossing without a physical barrier (e.g., gates in a lowered position) is not classified as a trespasser, even when the highway-rail grade crossing lights are activated or other warning systems are functioning. The person would be classified as a nontrespasser.

The term "suicide" is not defined in the Definitions section, but "suicide data" is defined later in the document in Section 6.3. Suicide Data and is depicted below:

Suicides and attempted suicides are no longer exceptions to FRA's reporting requirements and must be reported to FRA as "suicide data" on Form FRA 6180.55a when the casualty meets the general reporting criteria. Therefore, a railroad must evaluate the injury or fatality to determine whether it needs to create a report. Although self-inflicted wounds not inflicted for the purpose of committing suicide are still excluded (i.e., an employee intentionally cuts his hand without intending to kill himself). See § 225.15(c)(5).

Suicide data is data regarding the death of an individual due to that individual's commission of suicide as determined by a coroner, public police officer or other public authority; or injury to an individual due to that individual's attempted commission of suicide as determined by a public police officer or other public authority. A railroad police officer is not considered a public police officer within the meaning of the term. A public authority is a Federal, State, or local governmental agency with the legal authority to declare a casualty a suicide or an attempted suicide. Only the death of or injury to the individual who committed the suicidal act is considered to be suicide data. Therefore, an injury or fatality caused to a person by another person who committed suicide or attempted to commit suicide is not suicide data. For example, if the impact between the railroad on-track equipment and a highway user occurred because the highway user committed or attempted to commit suicide (as determined by a coroner, public police officer, or other public authority), the death of or injury to that highway user must be reported to FRA.

A railroad may accept verbal confirmation from the coroner, public police officer, or other public authority of the cause of the fatality or injury. Where a railroad receives verbal confirmation, it must document that confirmation in writing and create an audit trail so that FRA may confirm the cause of the casualty at a later time. The audit trail should include, but is not limited to, documentation of the name of the public police officer, coroner, or other public authority determining cause of death, his or her title, the date of confirmation, for whom the individual works, and the individual's telephone number and mailing address.

APPENDIX B. SIGNAGE PILOT STUDY (NINE MONTH)

A nine-month pilot study conducted by the Railroad Research Foundation (RRF), subcontracted to the American Association of Suicidology (AAS) attempted to evaluate the effectiveness of signage in preventing suicides on railroad rights of way.

Signs were posted along selected sections of track of the Long Island Railroad, New Jersey Transit, and Caltrain; each offered a message to individuals in suicidal or other crises to call a provided telephone number at a participating local crisis center.

During the nine-month study period, a total of 117 calls were made and received, 11 percent (N = 13) of which were from individuals who either volunteered or acknowledged in response to a question that they were thinking of or planning suicide. One railroad system accounted for 10 of the 13 suicidal calls made. Outcomes to these suicidal calls were, in general, positive and only one active intervention was made. Approximately two of every five calls were from individuals deemed to be in non-suicidal crises while the remaining 50 percent were calls that were unrelated to crises at all (e.g., requests for train schedules). Tragically, during the period of study there were 17 confirmed suicides along track mileage where project signage was installed and there was only a scant reduction (15 percent) in the number of suicides compared to the same 9-month period the prior year. However, no causal connection can be made between the introduction of signage and this observed reduction in the number of suicides while signage was in place.

Causal connections could not be made due to limitations of the study design. For example, the study lacked systematic signage installation so that a proper pre-post test could occur to validate the sign's presence as a countermeasure. Additionally, this initial pilot study only collected data for a 9-month study period; the amount of available data for analysis was too small to draw any meaningful conclusions.

Further study of signage is warranted, in which a more rigorous and systematic study design is implemented with factors that illustrate signage's effectiveness on railroad rights of way.

Appendix C. Ovenstone Criteria for Suicide on Railway Determination (UK)

The following is excerpted from the *Annual Safety Performance Report 2009/10: A Reference Guide to Safety Trends on GB Railways*, which was published by the RSSB in 2010.

Requirement:

Every railway fatality in Great Britain (including Scotland) is classified as:

- A suicide (that is, in accordance with the coroner's verdict – or Scottish equivalent),
- A suspected suicide (using the criteria provided), or
- Accidental.

A suspected/attempted suicide requires objective evidence of suicide (other than a coroner's verdict). It is a managerial assessment, based on applying the Ovenstone criteria adapted for the railways.

Without this positive evidence, the fatality should be deemed accidental. A classification should always be reviewed whenever new evidence comes to light (such as during investigations or at a coroner's inquest).

Whose Decision?

The classification is a matter for local railway management judgement, based on all available evidence (for example, eyewitness accounts of the person's behaviour – which may be the train driver's own account – BTP findings or the coroner's findings). The classification is wholly for management statistical purposes and is not:

- Passing judgement on the particulars of any case.
- For use outside the Railway Group.
- For any other purpose.

The Criteria for Suspected or Attempted Suicide

Each of the following, on its own, may be treated as sufficient evidence of suspected suicide (unless, of course, positive evidence that the fatality was accidental exists, or the coroner gives an accidental verdict):

- Suicide note.
- Clear statement of suicidal intent to an informant.
- Behaviour demonstrates suicidal intent.
- Previous suicide attempts.
- Prolonged depression.
- Instability; that is, a marked emotional reaction to recent stress or evidence of failure to cope (such as a breakdown).

APPENDIX D. CDC DETERMINATION OF SUICIDE: RECOMMENDATIONS

The following is excerpted from the *Medical Examiners' and Coroners' Handbook on Death Registration and Fetal Death Reporting*. This revision, published in 2003, is from the Center for Disease Control (CDC).

Pending investigation—used when determination of manner depends on further information. One of the more difficult tasks of the medical examiner or coroner is to determine whether a death is an accident or the result of an intent to end life. The medical examiner or coroner must use all information available to make a determination about the death. This may include information from his or her own investigation, police reports, staff investigations, and discussions with the family and friends of the decedent.

Determining a Suicide

There is evidence that death was self-inflicted. Pathological (autopsy), toxicological, investigatory, and psychological evidence, and statements of the decedent or witnesses, may be used for this determination.

There is evidence (explicit and/or implicit) that at the time of injury the decedent intended to kill self or wished to die and that the decedent understood the probable consequences of his or her actions.

- Explicit verbal or nonverbal expression of intent to kill self
- Implicit or indirect evidence of intent to die, such as the following:

  - Expression of hopelessness
  - Effort to procure or learn about means of death or rehearse fatal behavior
  - Preparations for death, inappropriate to or unexpected in the context of the
  - decedent's life
  - Expression of farewell or desire to die, or acknowledgment of impending death
  - Precautions to avoid rescue
  - Evidence that decedent recognized high potential lethality of means of death
  - Previous suicide attempt
  - Previous suicide threat
  - Stressful events or significant losses (actual or threatened)
  - Serious depression or mental disorder (10,11)

When Cause Cannot be Determined

It is well known that a professionally competent, searching autopsy and toxicological examination of the body fluids and organs, coupled with the best available bacteriologic, virologic, and immunologic studies, may fail to reveal the cause of death.

If this is the case and if the investigation has been pursued as far as possible, then the medical examiner or coroner will have no recourse but to indicate in one form or another that the cause of death ''Could not be determined.'' One possible phrase is ''Cause of death not determined at autopsy and toxicological examination.'' This is better than the term ''Unknown'' as it at least indicates the extent of the investigation undertaken.

Deferred "Pending Investigation"

Most, if not all, medical-legal investigative systems make provisions for cases in which the cause or manner of death cannot be immediately determined. Local laws vary somewhat as to how to handle such cases.

The procedure followed most frequently is to require that the death certificate be completed insofar as possible and filed within the time limits specified by law. Once the cause and/or manner of death are determined, a supplemental report must be prepared and filed by the medical-legal officer. This supplemental report becomes a part of the death certificate that is on file for the decedent.

ABBREVIATIONS AND ACRONYMS

AAS	American Association of Suicidology
CDC	Center for Disease Control
CFR	Code of Federal Regulations
CI	Confidence Interval
DOT	Department of Transportation
FRA	Federal Railroad Administration
FHWA	Federal High Way Administration
FY	Fiscal Year
HHS	Health And Human Services
HIOA	High Intensity Directed Acoustic
IASP	International Association for Suicide Prevention
KCR	Kowloon-Canton Railway
LED	Light-Emitting Diode
LIRR	Long Island Rail Road
LRAD	Low Range Acoustical Device
MBCR	Massachusetts Bay Commuter Railroad
MBTA	Massachusetts Bay Transit Authority
MDB	Mortality Database
MTR	Mass Transit Railway
NAMI	National Alliance of Mental Health
NNEPRA	Northern New England Passenger Railroad Authority
NJT	New Jersey Transit
NYSP	New Jersey Transit New York State Police
NY	New York

PED	Platform Edge Doors
PSD	Platform Screen Doors
RESTRAIL	Reduction of Suicides and Trespasses on Railway Property
ROW	Right of Way
RRF	Railroad Research Foundation
SAD	Seasonal Affective Disorder
SOS	Signs of Suicide
TTC	Toronto Transit
UK	United Kingdom
US	United States
WHO	World Health Organization
WMATA	Washington Metro Area Transit Authority

End Notes

[1] http://www.cdc.gov/nchs/fastats/suicide.htm. Last accessed on July 28, 2014.

[2] http://www.cdc.gov/nchs/fastats/suicide.htm. Last retrieved on 7/31/2014.

[3] Any incident that remains in the FRA database that was ruled a suicide is only available due to a railroad carrier's failure to remove the incident or possibly a technical glitch in the reporting system.

[4] FRA Guide for Preparing Accident/Incident Reports, May 23, 2011.

[5] This estimate is a minimum because it assumes that none of the 497 reported trespasser incidents were among the 268 suicides. This assumption is made because FRA does not require railroads to report suicides; however, it is possible that some suicides have been included. Additionally, it is likely that the 268 suicides were slightly under- sampled because of the difficult nature of collecting these data.

[6] This estimate is also likely to be low because of inconsistent reporting by railroads during the study timeframe. This inconsistent reporting led to an underestimation of the number of intentional acts during the study timeframe. Additionally, during the second timeframe (2007 – 2010), researchers stopped using media reports as a means to identify suicides on the railroad rights-of-way, thus reducing the ways by which suicides could be identified and/or verified.

[7] A suicide is *not* considered a trespasser if the individual is fatally struck at a grade crossing or other pedestrian crossing.

[8] FRA Guide for Preparing Accident/Incident Reports

[9] Calculated from the FRA Office of Safety Analysis Web site: http://safetydata.fra.dot.gov/OfficeofSafety/Default.aspx. Last accessed July 31, 2014.

[10] http://www.apta.com/resources/statistics/Documents/FactBook/APTA_2011_Fact_Book.pdf. Last retrieved August 4, 2014.

[11] http:// www.amtrak.com/ ccurl/ 730/658/FY13-Record-Ridership-ATK-13-122.pdf. Last retrieved August 4, 2014

[12] A hotspot location is defined as a region of track where multiple suicides have occurred over a brief timespan. The specifics of both the region of track and the timespan used to define the hotspot may vary depending on the purpose of the analysis. Hotspots may occur for trespassers in locations that are commonly used short cuts to illegally cross the right-of-way, or for suicides where a prior suicide may have elicited copycat acts.

[13] http://www.cdc.gov/violenceprevention/suicide/statistics/mechanism02.html. Last retrieved 7/30/2014.

[14] http://apps.who.int/iris/bitstream/10665/75166/1/9789241503570_eng.pdf. Last retrieved 8/1/2014.

[15] http://www.surgeongeneral.gov/library/reports/national-strategy-suicide-prevention/. Last retrieved 7/30/2014.

[16] This rate is substantially higher than in the United States. The population of Japan is roughly 40 percent lower than the population of the United States and the number of railway suicides is more than twice as high.

[17] http://seattletimes.com/html/nationworld/2008494010_bluelight11.html. Last retrieved 7/30/2014.

[18] Photograph taken by Elizabeth Machek of the Volpe National Transportation Systems Center in September 2012.

[19] http://en.rocketnews24.com/2012/02/29/could-cool-blue-lights-help-to-calm-the-suicidal/. Last retrieved July 30, 2014.

[21] http://www.metro.co.uk/news/world/762337-japan-installs-anti-suicide-blue-lights-at-railway-platforms. Last retrieved July 30, 2014.

[22] http://seattletimes.com/html/nationworld/2008494010_bluelight11.html. Last retrieved July 30, 2014.

[23] http://www.health.harvard.edu/newsletters/Harvard_Health_Letter/2012/May/blue-light-has-a-dark-side/. Last retrieved July 30, 2014.

[24] As confirmed through personal communications with two railroads currently using gatekeeper training programs to train station staff. The identities of these railroads cannot be released at this time.

[25] The Samaritans is a UK-based national charity that offers confidential emotional support services.

[26] http://www.samaritans.org/your-community/reducing-railway-deaths. Last accessed on July 30, 2014.

[27] http:// www.railcommunitysafety.com/ News/ Pages/ Barlaston-residents-given-specialist-training-to-stop-people- committing-suicide-on-railway-lines-near-their-homes.aspx. Last retrieved on July 30, 2014.

[28] http://www.bbc.co.uk/news/uk-20507106. Last retrieved on July 30, 2014.

[29] http://www.samaritans.org/media-centre/our-campaigns/were-your-corner. Last retrieved on July 30, 2014.

[30] Image taken from a City of Sunnyvale, CA, news report. A link to the report can be found here: http://sunnyvale.ca.gov/IntheCommunity/InTheCommunity/entryid/44.aspx. Last retrieved July 30, 2014.

[31] http:// www.ttc.ca/ News/ 2011/ June/ TTC_Distress_Centres_of_Toronto_Bell_Canada_ partner_suicide_.jsp. Last retrieved on July 31, 2014.

[32] http:// www.reuters.com/ article/ 2014/ 02/ 26/ us-usa-goldengate-suicides-idUSBREA1P03 Q20140226. Last retrieved on July 31, 2014.

[33] http://secondavenuesagas.com/2012/02/24/subway-related-deaths-account-for-7-of-nyc-suicides/. Last retrieved July 31, 2014.

[34] One of the recommendations in the media guidelines is to avoid using the term "suicide" in headlines; this guideline was followed for this report.

[35] http://www.brainysworld.com/. Last retrieved on March 19, 2014.

[36] Personal communication with several railroad representatives. Identities of the individuals and railroads will remain confidential to protect the anonymity of the railroads.

[37] http:// www.nj.com/ news/ index.ssf/ 2013/ 08/ deaths_on_nj_train_ tracks_increase_ since_state_ launched_safety_initiat ive.html. Last retrieved on July 31, 2014.

[38] FRA Railroad Trespassing Fact Sheet, December 2008

[39] The Railway Safety (Miscellaneous Provisions) Regulations 1997 requires railroads to ensure that unauthorized access to the railway by persons or animals is prevented. In 2011, the

Office of Rail Regulation (ORR) fined Network Rail £15,000 for failing to adequately maintain a trackside boundary fence in Whisby Nature Park, Lincolnshire (see http://orr.gov.uk/ August 1, 2014).data/ assets/ pdf_file/ 0018/ 5319/ prosecution-nr-180909.pdf Last retrieved

[40] https:// www.cia.gov/ library/ publications/the-world-factbook/fields/2121.html#us. Last retrieved on July 31, 2014.

[41] Images are from http://mic-ro.com/metro/platform-screen-doors.html. Last retrieved on August 1, 2014.

[42] http://today.14850.com/stories/05171-cornell-fences. Last retrieved on July 31, 2014.

[43] http://goldengate.org/news/NetSystemGrant.php. Last retrieved on July 31, 2014.

[44] Personal communication with railroad representative, September, 2012.

[45] Personal communication with railroad representative, September, 2013.

[46] http://www.lradx.com/site/content/view/285/110. Last retrieved on July 31, 2014.

[47] http://www.sdsheriff.net/newsroom/lrad.pdf. Last retrieved on July 31. 2014.

[48] Operation Lifesaver Train Safety FAQ: http://www.operationlifesaver.ca/facts-and-stats/train-safety-faq/. Last retrieved on July 31, 2014.

[49] Personal communication with commuter railroad representative, April 2012.

[50] Personal communication with commuter railroad representative, April 2012.

[51] Photo courtesy of Michael Martino.

[52] http:// www.maine.gov/ tools/whatsnew/ index.php?topic=DOT_ Press_Releases&id=602712 &v=article. Last retrieved on March 21, 2014.

[53] http://www.cnn.com/US/9612/30/gold.gate.suicide/. Last retrieved on July 31, 2014.

[54] http:// www.sfexaminer.com/ sanfrancisco/ saving-troubled-lives-just-part-of-gg-bridge-patrol/Content?oid=2337106. Last retrieved on July 31, 2014.

[55] *In 1994, the Hours of Service Act was repealed by Congress as part of a broad recodification of the Federal transportation laws. See Act of July 5, 1994, Pub. L. No. 103-272, 108 Stat. 745. The Act, which had been in Title 45, was repealed and recodified primarily as Chapter 211 of 49 U.S.C. Congress made clear that the recodification was not intended to make substantive changes in the affected laws, even though it altered their arrangement and language in certain respects. See Pub. L. No. 103-272, § 6(a), 108 Stat. 1378; H.R. Rep. No. 180, 103d Cong., 1st Sess. 1-5 (1993), reprinted in 1994 U.S. CODE CONG. & ADMIN. NEWS 818-822.*

In: Mitigating Suicides on Railways
Editor: Frances Diaz
ISBN: 978-1-63484-135-1

Chapter 2

DEFINING CHARACTERISTICS OF INTENTIONAL FATALITIES ON RAILWAY RIGHTS-OF-WAY IN THE UNITED STATES, 2007–2010*

Alan Berman, Ramya Sundararaman, Andrea Price, Karen Marshall, Michael Martino, Ann Doucette, Stephanie Chase and Scott Gabree

ABSTRACT

This report presents aggregate findings from 55 psychological autopsies of decedents who were identified as an intentional death (i.e., a suicide) on railroad rights-of-way between October 1, 2007, and September 30, 2010. The goal of this study was to assess whether there are unique characteristics of individuals involved in suicides on railroad rights-of-way compared with individuals who complete suicide by other means. The aggregate findings show that this sample of suicides on railroad rights-of-way share much in common with samples of suicides by other means. Only a few notable unique characteristics were found in the former population: the cases are more significantly marked by both

* This is an edited, reformatted and augmented version of a Technical Report, DOT/FRA/ORD-13/25, sponsored by the U.S. Department of Transportation, Federal Railroad Administration and issued May 2013.

severe mental disorder and substance abuse, the individuals tend to live near railroad tracks, and they are possibly less likely to have access to firearms. Additionally, the majority of these completed suicides occurred in urban or suburban areas as opposed to rural areas. The information collected for this effort may provide valuable information for the development of countermeasures or other intervention plans to mitigate this issue on railroad rightsof-way.

EXECUTIVE SUMMARY

Background

Completed suicides on railroad rights-of-way in the United States are relatively rare events; however, the impact on witnesses, discoverers, surviving loved ones, first responders, and railroad employees can be significant. In light of the consequences of these completed suicides to both the individuals involved and the railroads, identifying potential means to prevent these deaths would be beneficial. This study aims to assess whether individuals who complete suicide on railroad rights-of-way possess any unique characteristics that may help to inform the development of countermeasure or intervention strategies.

Methodology

To collect data about completed suicides on railroad rights-of-way in the United States, American Association of Suicidology (AAS) project investigators confirmed the determination of suicide as the cause of death; relevant data was gathered from medical examiner and coroner rulings and through psychological autopsy interviews with the decedents' next of kin. The psychological autopsy interviews involved a semi-structured interview protocol developed specifically for this study. Interviews were held with 165 next of kin and close friends to obtain information about 55 identified decedents.

Findings

The final study sample of 55 cases of suicide on the railroad right-of-way was found to be very similar to the known information about suicides by other means. Only a few factors seemed to differ from what would be expected from a suicide by other means. The identified decedents were generally found to be below the age of 50 and often had a last known address in close proximity to the railroad tracks. They were also more often described as having a mental disorder or substance abuse problem or both. Lastly, this sample was unlikely to have had access to a firearm. These factors appeared to influence the individuals' choice of this method to end his or her life.

Conclusion

Suicides on railroad rights-of-way have not been widely researched in the United States. This study revealed that individuals who complete suicide on the railroad rights-of-way share characteristics with individuals who complete suicide by other means. However, some differences were noted. Suicides on railroad rights-of-way involved higher proportions of younger individuals, according to national statistics provided by the Centers for Disease Control (CDC). Additionally, overall, decedents tended to have limited access to firearms (a more common means for completing suicide) and also tended to live near railroad tracks. The information detailed in this report can help in the development of a more strategic countermeasure approach. By better understanding the interacting characteristics of the individual and site at which these incidents occur, countermeasures can be developed and implemented in a more effective way.

1. Introduction

Trespassers on railroad rights-of-way have long been a serious issue for the railroad industry. As of the end of this data collection, the Federal Railroad Administration (FRA) does not track the number of completed suicides that occur each year; therefore, it is believed that a proportion of reported trespasser deaths are intentional (i.e., suicides).[1] When an individual takes his or her life on the railroad right-of-way, the effects on the railroad industry and its personnel are immense. By providing a better understanding of the characteristics and factors associated with individuals who intentionally choose to end their life in this manner, it is hoped that this study will aid in the development of effective countermeasures to reduce the frequency of these terrible events.

In a Research Results report by the FRA Office of Research and Development titled "Demographic Profile of Intentional Fatalities on Railway Rights-of-Way in the United States[2]," the researchers reported that a minimum of 25 percent and likely more than 35 percent of all fatalities on the railroad right-of-way are the result of an intentional act. They found that at least 268 completed suicides occurred on U.S. railroad rights-of-way between June 2006 and May 2007 (compared with 497 FRA reported trespasser fatalities during that same timeframe) and at least 428 completed suicides occurred on U.S. railroad rights-of-way between June 2007 and May 2010 (compared with 1,341 FRA reported trespasser fatalities during that same timeframe). The goal of the current report is to provide a more comprehensive understanding of the distinguishing factors that influence individuals who complete suicide on railroad rights-of-way.

1.1. Purpose

Completed suicides on railroad rights-of-way have not been widely researched in the United States. It is unknown whether individuals who complete suicide in this manner are uniquely affected by factors that may have little or no influence on individuals who complete suicide by other means. If the population of individuals who complete suicide on railroad rights-of-way is different from those who complete suicide by other means, then intervention strategies which specifically target these individuals may need to be developed. This study aims to assess whether there are indeed unique characteristics influencing or affecting individuals who complete suicide on railroad rights-of-way rather than by other means. The results of the study may inform future countermeasure or intervention strategies and perhaps dissuade individuals from this course of action.

1.2. Definitions

For the purposes of this study, a railroad will be defined as follows using Railway Age's Comprehensive Railroad Dictionary:

1. All forms of non-highway ground transportation that runs on rails, including freight transportation using locomotives and freight cars; commuter or other short-haul rail-passenger service in metropolitan or suburban areas; high-speed ground transportation systems that connect metropolitan areas, without regard to whether they use new technologies not associated with traditional railroads. This term does not include rapid transit operations within an urban area that are not connected to the railroad system of transportation.
2. A system of railroad track including the land, stations, rolling stock, and other related property.

The title of this document does not include the term "suicide" and instead states "Intentional Fatalities." This is because existing voluntary media guidelines suggest that using the term "suicide" in a headline may actually increase the likelihood of copycat incidents.[3] Accordingly, members of the media should take heed if considering publishing any information included in this report and reference the corresponding media guidelines. However, since the term "suicide" is widely used in the past research discussed within this paper, and well understood, the term suicide will not be replaced in the body of this report.

1.3. Background

This is the first study that focuses on whether there are characteristics, risk factors, and warning signs unique to individuals who complete suicide on railroad rights-of-way in the United States, in contrast to individuals who complete suicide by other means. Previous research on this topic has primarily been conducted outside the United States (Ladwig & Baumert, 2004; Mishara, 1999). Work conducted within the United States has been limited to epidemiological or demographic information (Botha, et al., 2010). In addition, studies such as the one by Botha, et al. are based primarily on highly urbanized railroad systems, with no clear discrimination between freight, commuter, and transit lines. While commuter and transit lines are mostly in urban and suburban areas, freight tracks also cover rural areas which are known to experience different types of health concerns, for example, higher rates of substance abuse and lower likelihood of treatment (Eberhardt, Ingram, Mkuc, et al, 2001). These findings highlight key patterns regarding completed suicides on each type of track.

Although most studies have been conducted only on urbanized stretches of railroad, they still provide a baseline estimate of the age and gender of the decedents involved in railroad right-of-way suicides. A Danish study by Lindekilde and Wang (1985) found that 44 percent of those who completed suicide on railroad rights-of-way were between 15 and 29 years old, while only 11 percent of those who completed suicide by other means were in this age group. Kerkhof (2003) noted that in the Netherlands most suicides on the railway involved men between 20 and 29 years old. And Botha et al. (2010) found that suicides on the Caltrain commuter rail system were 3.5 times more likely among men than women.

The Suicides and Open Verdicts on the Railway Network (SOVRN) Project, commissioned in 1999 in the United Kingdom, used data from investigations by coroners and case study interviews to identify characteristics of individuals who completed suicide on the railroad over a 3-year period (N = 103) (Abbott, Young, Grant, Goward, Seaward, & Pugh, 2003). The study found demographic results relatively similar to those cited above: the decedents in this study were typically male (the male-to-female ratio is approximately 4:1) and half of the decedents were between 16 and 40 years old. In addition, this study was able to go beyond basic demographic data to provide information about potential risk factors that led to each individual's suicide and, in some cases, specific information about the decision to complete this act on the railroad right-of-way.

Using coronial investigations and psychological autopsies, the SOVRN project was able to characterize decedents as being unemployed (37 percent), living alone (25 percent), and living with a physical condition (26 percent). Additionally, for whom this information could be gathered, 76 percent of the decedents had been diagnosed with a mental health condition at the time of death (and 29 percent of those decedents had been diagnosed with an additional, secondary mental health condition).

Like the SOVRN project, the current research does not rely solely on coroner and police reports to gather information about decedents. The psychological autopsy method used in this report allowed researchers to collect information about each decedent that goes beyond typical demographic data. A psychological autopsy allows a researcher to obtain information about the likely mental and physical state of an individual who dies by suicide, as well as the relevant characteristics of their environment and location of death (Cavenagh, Carson, Sharpe, & Lawrie, 2003).

1.4. Psychological Autopsy

In 1958, Edwin Shneidman, Norman Farberow, and Robert Litman—then directors of the Los Angeles Suicide Prevention Center—coined the term "psychological autopsy." These clinician-researchers, working in collaboration with the Los Angeles County Medical Examiner's Office, devised a set of procedures to assist the medical examiner (ME) in medico-legal investigations for cases where the ME could not readily determine the manner of death (suicide, homicide, accident, or natural). Since then, the psychological autopsy has evolved into a systematic "tool" for collecting retrospective psychological and related data about a decedent through semi-structured interviews with knowledgeable informants (typically family members, friends, and coworkers or classmates) and analyses of archived documents and records of the decedent's life (e.g., health records, criminal records). Where deaths have clearly been determined to be suicides, the psychological autopsy can potentially identify distal (lifetime) and proximate (near term) risk factors. (Note: distal and proximate are the terms used by the psychological autopsy community). When conducted with trained researchers and a standardized protocol, a psychological autopsy has the potential to yield reliable and valid data (Kelly & Mann, 1996; Brent, Perper, Mortiz, Allman, Roth, Schweers, & Balach, 2007).

Although data collected from psychological autopsies are seen as useful to researchers, it is important to note that the data cannot be objectively validated for several reasons (which are detailed in the limitations section of this report). One most obvious limiting factor is that the findings cannot be confirmed by the decedent; therefore, the results presented in this report will focus primarily on factual information (e.g., employment status) and not discuss other more subjective findings (e.g., the victim was acting more reckless). For example, a suicide which appeared to be impulsive to one next of kin may have been perceived by another informant as planned; this subjectivity leads to an increase in the potential for error in the sample. In the current study, aggregate findings from these psychological autopsies were used to provide a basic understanding of modal factors within the decedents life and to better understand why suicides occur on railroad rights-of-way (in contrast to other available and accessible methods). The study discussed in this paper is the first documented psychological autopsy study of suicides on the railroad rights-of-way in the United States.

2. Methodology

2.1 Overview

The current study uses a psychological autopsy, which utilizes a semi-structured interview approach, to investigate factors associated with an individual who has completed suicide. The psychological autopsy is used as a tool to reconstruct a decedent's life in order to understand the causes, mechanisms, and, if undetermined, the mode or manner of death. It relies primarily on the identification and cooperation of knowledgeable informants, typically next of kin. For the current study, researchers developed a specific protocol for collecting data about individuals who complete suicide on railroad system rights-of-way in the United States. The protocol will be described in the following sections. Limitations of the protocol will be discussed in the conclusion of this section (section 2.6).

2.2. Case Identification

Four hundred sixty six (466) cases were identified as completed suicides on railroad rights-of-way in the United States during the 36-month timeframe of October 1, 2007, through September 30, 2010. For each of the 466 cases, the representative medical examiner or coroner was contacted to verify that the manner of death was determined to be a suicide.[4] A copy of the decedent's death certificate was received in 237 (51 percent) of the cases. Some discrepancy between suspected suicides and those corroborated by medical examiners is not uncommon and is largely due to such issues as differential thresholds of interpreting evidence and relationships between law enforcement and clinicians (Timmermans, 2005). For each of the 237, an attempt was made to contact the decedent's next of kin and close friends and ask them to participate in this study for the purpose of learning more about what factors may have been influential in the completed suicide. Contact information was available for 182 of the 237 total cases.

2.3. Contacting Informants

From information contained in the medical examiner or coroner reports, data elements were compiled. These elements consist of personal and demographic information about the deceased (e.g., home address, age, gender, ethnicity), as well as the date and time, manner, and location of the death. This information, along with additional data found through public sources (e.g., memorials, social networking sites), was used to identify the next of kin and other individuals potentially knowledgeable about the decedent.

To allow time for next of kin, friends, and coworkers of the decedent to move past the initial shock of the death being investigated, attempts to recruit them for participation occurred after a minimum of 6 months had passed since the death had been ruled a suicide.[5] Initial contact consisted of a packet including a project description and a letter of introduction identifying the researcher as the official performer of this Railroad Research Foundation and Federal Railroad Administration (RRF and FRA) funded research. The project information packet was followed up by a telephone call placed by the research team staff to request a face-to-face meeting for the interview. If the next of kin agreed to participate, an investigator contacted the next of kin to arrange a meeting. At the time of consent, the nature of the study and potential risks and benefits were discussed. Potential interviewees were given time to ask questions and were offered a summary of the research protocol. Interviewees were asked to sign a consent form. Interviewers emphasized the message that had been already transmitted in the initial telephone contact: that a respondent could stop the interview at any time. Family members or friends who were unable to respond to questions regarding the informed consent procedure were excluded from the study. To identify additional family and friends for interviews, the next of kin were asked if there were any friends, teachers, coworkers, or significant others that they felt could provide further information.

In deciding the number of informants to be interviewed for each case, the project followed guidance offered by the U.S. Surgeon General's *National Strategy for Suicide Prevention* which states that for every suicide, there are six to eight individuals who have been closely associated with the decedent (U.S. Department of Health and Human Services, 2001). The goal of the current study was to interview up to eight informants per case, unless conflicting reports from the first eight informants necessitated additional interviews. The selection of informants was based on their presumed knowledge of the decedent (using criteria such as proximity, duration, and relationship with decedent) and of the events leading up to his or her death.

Investigators stopped soliciting additional interviews when one of the two scenarios listed below occurred. Investigators strived to accomplish the first scenario whenever possible, but would resort to the second scenario when necessary:

1. All the questions in the protocol were answered and multiple informants corroborated the responses.
2. Discussions with next of kin or other informants revealed no other informants who were willing to be interviewed or who had any further information about the decedent.

A final sample of 55 cases is included in this report. Table 1 summarizes the process leading to the final selection. The final sample was derived from the 466 total identified cases of which 237 were confirmed as suicides by autopsy or death certificate. Of the 237 cases which were determined to be a completed suicide, AAS project staff found contact information for next of kin in 182 cases. Next of kin in 69 cases agreed to be interviewed and interviews were scheduled in 63 of those cases. In 36 of the 182 cases, the next of kin refused participation and in 77 cases no response was received. Although 63 cases were scheduled, funding constraints allowed only 61 cases to be completed. The remaining two cases were cancelled and appropriate outreach was extended to these individuals by the AAS project coordinator. Interviews for each case were generally conducted over a 2-week period, depending on the respondents' availability.

Table 1. Derivation of Study Sample from Total Identified Completed Suicides on Railroad Rights-of-Way

Description	Number
Total identified cases between October 1,2007,and September 30, 2010	466
Total confirmed cases	237
Number of cases sent letters	182
Number of cases for which there was no reply	77
Number of potential cases that refused to participate	36
Number who consented	69
Number of cases with scheduled interviews	63
Number of cases interviewed	61
Completed cases that did not meet quality screen of being able to answer the research questions outlined in Section 3	6
Final Sample of cases	55

2.4. Interview Process

A total of 165 informants provided data, resulting in a mean of 3 informants and a range of 2 to 9 informants per case. The maximum time period between the suicide and the interview was two years and the minimum was six months. Before conducting the interviews, next of kin and other informants were asked to review and sign a consent form to indicate that they were aware that the data would be held confidential and that they had the right to withdraw from the interview at any time. The nature of the study and potential risks and benefits were discussed in greater detail. Next of kin were also asked to sign a standard written authorization for AAS project staff to obtain the decedent's health records from healthcare providers. For all the cases, next of kin provided this authorization. However, despite authorization, no healthcare providers returned calls; therefore, none provided the requested information regarding treatment provided to the decedent.

Interviews were conducted by one investigator with each informant individually. When family members felt strongly that they needed another family member to support them through the interview the investigator conducted the interview with both family members, however, this did not happen frequently. At the end of each interview, the investigator provided the informant with support information such as a list of support groups in the local area. Of the 165 informants, 29 accepted the contact information for mental health therapy or treatment. There was no further follow-up to determine whether the informants actually sought help.

The investigator relied on handwritten notes taken during the interview. Investigators made every attempt to verify the information provided by the informants by seeking corroboration from other informants and asking for evidence where appropriate. The investigators' final assessment for each case was reviewed by the principal investigator and research director for quality control. When the assessments were reviewed, it was determined that in six cases, the quality of information obtained from the informants was insufficient to adequately understand the circumstances leading to the suicide, and no further informants were available for those cases. All information was maintained by the AAS project coordinator with documents identified by ID number and locked in a secure area.

2.5. Investigator Training

Investigators were required to have a background in the social sciences (although not all were psychologists) and were trained for this study to identify and deal therapeutically with any possible negative psychological consequences from the interview. Upon selection as an investigator for this project, and before being assigned a case, every investigator received 12 hours of training from the principal investigator and research director in supportive interviewing techniques. In the training, investigators were provided information about psychological autopsy studies, the study methodology, and background. They were trained in how to obtain information for each question on the semi-structured protocol and were asked to role-play the interview. In addition, when half of the cases had been completed, each investigator received 16 hours of updated training, based on the experience gained through this study, to refine their interviewing and data collection skills. During this updated training, investigators built on their practical knowledge in responding to commonly encountered challenges and in data reporting so as to minimize additional questions during case review with the principal investigator and research director.

2.6. Methodological Limitations

Although psychological autopsy is recognized as a "best practice" tool for establishing possible causal factors leading to suicides, it is not without known limitations. One limitation is the lack of control over the informants chosen for the study. Although researchers were able to eliminate informants who were deemed to be untrustworthy or not knowledgeable enough about the individual in question, the procedures of the psychological autopsy cannot ensure that all informants are equally knowledgeable about the decedent or that approximately the same amount of time has passed between the decedent's death and each of the interviews. As such, the depth of knowledge that can be obtained about each decedent is likely to vary. As noted earlier, some inconsistency is to be expected in the interpretation of the decedent's thoughts, emotions, and motivations. Therefore, we purposefully chose to focus on the more objective information (e.g., employment, criminal or legal status, etc.) as opposed to estimating the subjective information as judged by the informants (e.g., the decedent's emotional state)

3. RESULTS

The final study sample consists of 55 cases, as shown in Table 1. Each case consists of one decedent and a varying number of interviewed informants. In the following section, demographic characteristics of each decedent are presented, followed by additional objective data collected by investigators during the psychological autopsy interviews.

3.1. Demographic Characteristics

Gender. The final sample of 55 cases was composed of 9 (16 percen females and 46 (84 percent) males. This distribution is similar to that of completed suicide reports on the railroad rights-of-way and for U.S. suicid by all means from 2007 to 2010 (see Table 2 ($\chi^2 = 0.748$, df=1, P>0.05).

Age. The median age of the 55 psychological autopsied cases was years. The distribution of ages showed that 18 (33 percent) decedents w under the age of 30, 22 (40 percent) decedents were between the ages of and 50, and 15 (27 percent) decedents were 51 years old or older. comparison, the age distribution for suicides by any means in the United St shows that 31,416 (22 percent) of the decedents are under the age of 30 58,880 (40 percent) of decedents are 51 years old or older. The sample for study may appear to have fewer older individuals than would be expe given the national statistics noted in Table 2 below; however, a chi square of significance did not reveal a significant difference ($\chi^2 = 5.59$, df=2, p>(Additionally, it is worth noting that the distribution of ages from the samp psychological autopsies differed from the age distribution of all rep suicides on the railroad right-of-way that occurred during the same time f Therefore, the appearance of an over representation of younger victims in the psychological autopsied cases is likely to only be an artifact limited sample size and not a true age bias.

Table 2 shows the distribution of gender and age as a percentage o different groups: first, the sample of 55 cases included in this study; the total number of completed suicides reported during this study durati third, the total number of suicides by all means in the United States b January 1, 2007, and December 31, 2010.[6]

Table 2. Comparison of Gender and Age of Study Population, Confirmed Cases, and U.S. Suicides

Characteristic	Cases included in Psychological Autopsy study 10/2007–9/2010 (% of N = 55)	All reported suicides identified by the study 10/2007–9/2010 (% of N = 466)	U.S. suicides by all means 1/2007–12/2010 (% of N = 145,906)
Male	84	81	79
Female	16	19	21
Age <30 years	33	18	22
Age 31–50 years	40	47	38
Age >50 years	27	35	40

Race. In the initial study sample of 466, only 262 reported race. Of the cases that reported race, the majority of the decedents were white, 209 (88 percent). Of the 55 cases included in this sample 53 (96 percent) were white. Seven percent of the confirmed cases and two percent of the autopsied cases were black, and the remainder was composed of other races. This finding is also consistent with suicides in general[7]; the CDC reports that 91 percent of suicide decedents were white and 6 percent were black.[8]

Sexual Orientation. Based on information provided for only 52 decedents for whom sexual orientation was reported, more than 90 percent (approximately 47 of the decedents) were believed to be straight, compared to fewer than 5 individuals who were known to be gay, lesbian, bisexual, or transgender. Although there is no comparable and consistent national data to compare with regards to suicide by all means, a comparable 7% of women and 8% of men identify as gay, lesbian or bisexual; therefore the distribution of sexual orientations found in this study sample were not very different from the overall national population (Reece, Herbenick, Fortenberry, Dodge, Sanders, & Schick, 2010).

Marital Status and Offspring. Of the 55 decedents, 31 (56 percent) were single and never married (but not cohabitating), 11 (20 percent) were divorced or separated, and 8 (15 percent) were married at the time of their death. Less than five individuals were widowed (and not married, divorced, or separated) or cohabitating. One out of four of the single, never married individuals had experienced a recent breakup. Although recent national surveillance data are not available for comparison, a 1988 study that analyzed overall U.S. suicide rates over a 3-year period found that 47 percent were married, 29 percent were

single, 9 percent were widowed, and 15 percent were divorced (Smith, Mercy, & Conn, 1988).

Only 19 (35 percent) of the decedents in the current study sample had children: 6 (11 percent) decedents had one child, 7 (13 percent) decedents had two children, and 6 (11 percent) decedents had more than two children.

3.1.1. Geographic Distribution

To better understand the location of all reported completed suicides on railroad rights-ofway, a map of the United States is presented below to illustrate the distribution of these cases. Figure 1 shows the distribution of confirmed completed suicides on railroad rights-of-way (blue markers) along with the distribution of cases autopsied in this study (red plus signs). It is important to note that each blue marker may represent more than one case if multiple suicides occurred on the railroad right-of-way in a single city within the study period. Therefore, it is impossible from this map to get an accurate picture of where the most completed suicides occurred in the United States. However, a visual comparison of the two sets of markers shows some similarity between the nationwide distribution of all confirmed cases and the sample. The only notable omissions in the current sample seem to be the Northwest United States and portions of the lower Midwest (e.g., Arkansas, Tennessee, and Kentucky), where several confirmed suicides occurred on railroad rights-of-way but was not included in the study sample.

3.1.2. Employment

Of the decedents in this study, 49 (90 percent) had at least some high school education, 26 (47 percent) had at least some college education, and fewer than five decedents were full-time students at the time of their death. Fourteen (25 percent) decedents were known to have full-time employment at the time of death, and eight (15 percent) were known to have part-time employment.

Of the decedents, fewer than five were full-time students so their employment status was not included in the data sample Of the remaining 51 decedents, 22 (43 percent) were known to have full- or part-time employment. Of those with an employment history, only 9 (19 percent) held professional jobs, such as educator or division manager, 13 (27 percent) had worked in the service industry, 12 (25 percent) had histories as laborers, and 6 (13 percent) performed temporary jobs.

Blue markers and red crosses indicate all the confirmed suicide cases on railroad rights-of-way; red crosses indicate the cases included in our study sample. Map of the United States. Retrieved on Aug 21, 2007, from http://maps.google.com.

Figure 1. Geographic Distribution of Confirmed Suicides on Railroad Rights-ofWay (N = 237) and Study Sample (N = 55).

3.1.3. Government System Involvement

Of the 53 cases for which this information was available, 25 (47 percent) were involved with a nonmedical social system, such as the welfare system or the criminal justice system, at the time of their death. Eight (15 percent) of the decedents were involved with the legal system at the time of the suicide and five of these cases involved upcoming court dates following arrest for driving under the influence of alcohol.

3.1.4. Mental and Physical Disorder

Mental Disorder. A mental disorder is a health condition characterized by significant dysfunction in an individual's cognitions, emotions, or behaviors that reflects a disturbance in the psychological, biological, or developmental processes underlying mental functioning.[9] Mental disorders are diagnosed according to criteria that present in the form of symptoms, feelings, thoughts, or behaviors either observable to or reported by the individual to others. Since no medical providers responded to the researchers' requests for formal diagnoses, the research team used informant interviews to determine the presence of a mental or physical disorder in the decedent. For this study the criteria used by the research team to confirm a mental disorder as present in the decedent were that an interviewed informant reported a previous diagnosis made by a professional *or* the interviewee had evidence of prescriptions, medical records or other records to provide to the investigator to confirm the diagnosis.

Mental disorder is a known risk factor for suicide and has been reported to exist in approximately 90 percent of all adult suicides (Phillips, 2010; Cavanaugh, Carson & Sharpe, 2003; Tanney, 2000). The results of this study suggest that the rate of mental disorder among the cases studied may be even higher; 53 (96 percent) of the total 55 cases were reported to have a mental disorder. Informants reported that 25 (47 percent) had been prescribed medications for their mental disorder, and 12 (23 percent) were in therapy. Of the 25 who had been prescribed medications, informants indicated that 10 (40 percent) were taking the medications as prescribed; only 5 of those 10 reported the medication as effective.

Few studies have investigated the prevalence of mental disorders among decedents of completed suicides on the railroad rights-of-way. One such study out of Queensland, Australia, reported that approximately 40 percent of individuals in a 15-year span of completed suicides on railroad rights-of-way had a mental disorder (De Leo & Krysinska, 2008). Another study in the Netherlands reported that 53 percent of the 57 cases studied were in psychiatric care at the time of their suicide, and two-thirds were in inpatient care (Houwelingen & Kerkhof, 2008). This study is just one example of an oft-cited finding in European studies suggesting that railroad suicide deaths frequently occur at railroad track sites within just a few kilometers of psychiatric hospitals (Houwelingen, Kerkhof, & Beersma, 2010).

Also noted in this sample of 55 cases is that 40 (73 percent) of these cases were reported to have two or more co-occurring diagnoses. Among those with reported co-occurring mental disorders, only 10 (25 percent) were in therapy at the time of death. Twenty-one (53 percent) had reportedly been prescribed medications for their conditions at the time of death. Only 9 (43 percent) of the individuals who had been prescribed medications for co-occurring mental disorders were reported to be taking their medications as prescribed at the time of death. Further, informants revealed that the medications prescribed were perceived to be effective for fewer than half of the individuals reported as being compliant with their prescriptions.

During the interview process, interviewers also asked informants about the decedent's emotional and psychological condition leading up to the incident. Although a reliable account of the specifics of the decedent's emotional and psychological condition may not be possible to ascertain through this process, it was clear to the investigators that most decedents suffered from severe emotional or psychological distress in the time leading up to the suicide.

In some cases, the family of the decedent had a history of mental illness. Thirty-five (64 percent) decedents were reported to have had a family member with a mental disorder. For 17 of those individuals, at least one of their parents had a mental disorder, and in 13 cases, at least one sibling.

A family history of suicide exposes the vulnerable individual to a model that has the potential to influence and impel suicidal behaviors. Nineteen decedents (35 percent) had a family history of suicide. Moreover, a family history may indicate a genetic or biochemical vulnerability to suicide.

Physical Disorder. For some individuals, physical illness underlies their decision to end their life by suicide. Lung disease, Acquired Immune Deficiency Syndrome (AIDS), and ulcers, among others, have all been seen to be associated with a significantly increased likelihood of suicide attempt, independent of the effects of mental disorders (Goodwin, Marusic, & Hoven, 2003).

Twenty-eight (51 percent) decedents in this study had at least one chronic physical illness. Chronic physical illnesses reported by informants included diabetes (7), chronic pain (5), and less than five cases each of cardiovascular disease, endocrine disorders other than diabetes, brain injury, and asthma. Medical conditions such as these have long been recognized as risk factors for suicide (Berman & Pompili, 2011).

3.1.5. Substance Abuse and Toxicology Reports

Substance abuse, or the abuse of alcohol, use of illicit drugs, or abuse of prescription medications, is a known risk factor (both acute and lifetime) for suicide (Center for Substance Abuse Treatment, 2008). All decedents in this study were reported to have abused substances, to have had a mental disorder, or both. Among the study sample, 34 decedents (62 percent) were reported to have been heavy consumers of alcohol, and 32 decedents (58 percent) were reported to have been abusing drugs (these two groups overlap). Among the decedents who were reported to have abused substances, all except two also had a mental disorder. According to the CDC, 16.5 percent of U.S. individuals who completed suicide between 2003 and 2004 had alcohol dependence problems.

Toxicology reports with Blood Alcohol Content (BAC) at the time of death were available for 43 (78 percent) decedents. At the time of death, 22 of the 43 (51 percent) cases had positive readings: blood alcohol content (16), illicit drugs (7), or prescription drugs (7). The most frequently abused illicit drugs were marijuana (5) and cocaine (fewer than 5). It was also found that a single individual had positive readings for more than one substance. Of the 16 decedents who had been drinking at the time of their death, 15 had a BAC above the statutory legal limit for driving a vehicle in most states (.08).

3.1.6. Precipitating Factors

In many suicides, a triggering event—one single event or series of events—leads that individual to attempt to take his or her life (Moscicki, 1997). These events, by themselves, are not sufficient to lead a healthy person to end his or her life. However, to a person who has become vulnerable to suicide, the event or set of events triggers the suicide. Existing research on suicide attempters cite precipitating factors including academic stress, chronic physical illness, death of a loved one, economic distress, family and intimate partner relationship problems, occupational stress, substance abuse, and unemployment (Wu, Su & Chen, 2009; Beautrais, 1997). These factors were among those being experienced by decedents according to interviewees in the current study.

In 51 (94 percent) of 55 cases, the decedents were believed to have been experiencing at least one known stressful or adverse event. In 19 (35 percent) cases, it was fear of an upcoming negative or humiliating event, such as a court hearing, an expectation of incarceration, or loss of custody of children. Additionally, it was found that 8 (15 percent) had experienced the dissolution of a relationship with a significant other in the weeks or months prior to their death. In fewer than five cases, no precipitating factors were identified.

3.1.7. Past Attempts

The most significant predictor of a future suicide is a past suicide attempt (Runeson, Tidemalm, Dahlni, Lichtenstein, & Langstrom, 2010). Results of this study show that 24 (44 percent) decedents attempted suicide at least once in the past. Some decedents, using both high and low lethality methods, had attempted suicide multiple times.[10] Of the decedents who had made one or more known prior suicide attempts, 19 (79 percent) had used at least one low lethality method (e.g., ingestion pills, poison) and 11 (46 percent) had used at least one high lethality method (e.g., jumping). Almost half (5) of the individuals who made a high lethality prior suicide attempt had tried, in that prior attempt, to end their lives on railroad rights-of-way.

It should be noted that some individuals who are involved in incidents on the railroad rights-of-way do not die from these incidents. According to FRA, on average, 900 individuals are struck annually by trains while trespassing on the railroad rights-of-way. Of these trespasser incidents, approximately half result in a fatality. As Figure 2 indicates, not all attempts to end one's life on the railroad rights-of-way result in a fatality. It is important to note that this graph includes all trespasser events (intentional and unintentional), so it is unclear what percentage of the intentional acts resulted in a fatality. Ultimately, being struck by a train does not necessarily result in a fatality. Also, this study did not investigate known attempts that did not end in a fatality. Examining the occurrence of known attempts that did not result in a fatality may uncover important information about why these attempts were made, however, funding did not allow for this investigation to be performed.

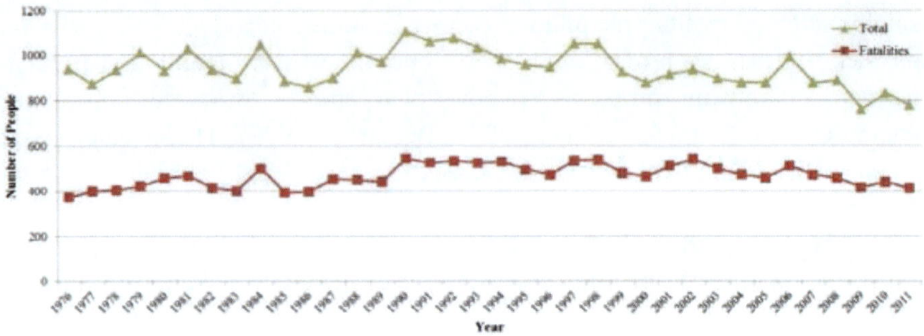

Figure 2. Trespasser Incidents vs. Trespasser Fatalities [11, 12, 13]

3.1.8. Characteristics of the Suicide

Witnesses. A completed suicide on the railroad right-of-way can be a very public event, depending on the site and time of day the death occurred. Completed suicides on railroad rights-of-way are categorized by Symonds, as private (likely not witnessed) or public (likely witnessed) (Symonds, 1994). In the United Kingdom, 64 percent of completed suicides on railroad rights-of-way occur in public settings, while only one-third occur in a secluded environment. A completed suicide at a station platform is almost always witnessed by passengers and railroad personnel.

In this study, 54 of the 55 cases occurred on open track away from a train station. In one case, the decedent was witnessed stepping off the platform. Of the cases that occurred away from a station, informants reported that 23 (42 percent) decedents had been observed by members of the community in the vicinity of the site of their death within 30 minutes before their death. While most completed suicides on railroad rights-of-way are witnessed by the train engineers, among the individuals studied, the actual event was only directly witnessed by bystanders in 6 (11 percent) cases.

Time of Day. An individual who attempts suicide on the railroad right-of-way during daylight hours may increase the chances of being seen and possibly rescued. The suicides in this sample occurred most frequently in afternoons and early evenings. Though daylight hours vary significantly across the country and at different times of year it is likely that for a fair proportion of these deaths, there was the possibility for the incident to be witnessed. This means that with increased monitoring, it may have been possible for these suicides to have been prevented. However, as noted above, only 6 of these 55 cases were witnessed by an observer, suggesting that decedents, for the most part, took precautions to avoid being seen. The analysis of incidents by time of day was performed in an earlier demographics profile study and no pattern emerged (FRA, 2011).

Behavior on Tracks. Completed suicides on railroad rights-of-way can be characterized as follows: jumpers (those who leap in front of an approaching train), liers or prostraters (those who lie across the tracks awaiting a train), or wanderers (those who walk on the train tracks). This information was collected for 50 of the 55 cases in the study. According to the data, 20 (36 percent) of the decedents were categorized as liers, 15 (27 percent) were jumpers, and 15 (27 percent) decedents were wanderers who faced the train directly. In the *SOVRN* study, the most common behaviors were standing on the track (wanderers) followed by jumping in front of the train.

3.1.9. Personal Possessions at Time of Death

Reports on decedents' possessions at the time of death were available in 29 of 55 cases or 52 percent of the study sample. In 7 (24 percent) of these cases, decedents had no possessions with them. In 9 (31 percent) cases, decedents had their wallet or purse with their identification. Fewer than five decedents were reported to have a cell phone with them.

The lack of a cell phone may suggest that any prevention program focused on displaying signage to encourage suicidal individuals to call a dedicated suicide prevention call center would need to include a dedicated telephone and not presume that the individual had a cell phone in his or her possession. However, informants anecdotally reported some instances where the decedent had visited the railroad tracks prior to the actual incident, which, in theory, provides multiple opportunities to see the sign and make the call from another telephone.

When left, notes can offer a glimpse into the mindset of the decedent in the hours or days preceding the suicide, when—it is presumed—these notes are written. In this sample, 16 (29 percent) left a suicide note, which is in line with the findings of 33 percent of those who die by suicide by all means (Haines, Williams, & Lester, 2011). Fewer than five of these individuals had the note on their person, while the remaining notes were around elsewhere, e.g., in the decedents home, car, or near the site.

3.1.10. Site Accessibility and Significance

Investigators were able to explore the characteristics of the sites in 52 (95 percent) of 55 cases. Of the cases in the study sample, 46 (84 percent) occurred on stretches of track that did not have a barrier to restrict access to the railroad right-of-way. Investigators were asked to characterize each site relative to its density[14] (i.e., number of buildings versus open space) on a 3-point scale from low to high density.[15] Of the cases studied, based on the subjective classification of sites, 27 (49 percent) occurred in a high density area, 13 (24 percent) in an area of medium density, and 15 (27 percent) in an area of low density. Additionally, investigators were asked to classify these sites as rural, suburban, or urban.[16] It was subjectively reported that 11 completed suicides (20 percent) occurred in rural areas, 30 (55 percent) occurred in suburban residential areas, and 14 (25 percent) occurred in urban areas. These findings indicate that the majority of these completed suicides occurred in or near high density, metropolitan, or suburban areas (population centers).

Additionally, of the 46 cases for which site characteristics were available, 40 (87 percent) of the decedents lived within 2 miles of the incident site—and 35 (76 percent) of these decedents lived less than 1 mile from the incident site.[17]

3.1.11. Availability of Firearms

In the United States, the most common method for suicide is the use of a firearm.[18] The majority of suicides are the result of the use of a firearm (50.8 percent of all suicides in 2009). In many instances, if a firearm is readily accessible in the home, the individual intending to complete suicide by firearm will die at home (Maris, Berman, and Silverman, 2000). Current estimates indicate that firearms are owned by roughly 38 percent of U.S. households (Hepbum, Miller, Azrael & Hemmenway, 2007).

Informants were asked if the decedent had ready access to a firearm and ammunition. For the purposes of this study "having access to a firearm" was defined as being able to obtain a firearm (your own or another individual's) and use it to end one's life. Among the study sample, informants reported that 12 (22 percent) decedents had access to a firearm and still chose to complete suicide on the railroad right-of-way. It is notable that this proportion is less than expected, given the proportion of U.S. households owning a firearm. However, it is worth noting that the total number of non-firearm suicides who did in fact have access to a firearm, a potentially more meaningful comparison group, is not currently known. Although we do not know how accessible firearms were to the decedent, the decision to complete suicide on a railroad right-of-way may have been at least partially dictated by the absence of a more lethal alternate means.

4. Discussion

The goal of this study is to assess whether there are unique factors that affect or influence individuals who complete suicide on railroad rights-of-way compared with suicides by other means. If such characteristics do exist, that information may inform future countermeasure or intervention strategy development.

As described in Section 3, the psychological autopsy protocol aimed to identify characteristics of individuals who complete suicide on railroad rights-of-way. In general, the characteristics of the decedents in this study were very similar to characteristics known about decedents who used other methods of suicide. Still, there are a few pieces of information that stand out as possible differences with this population:

- Many of the decedents in this study had a last known address in close proximity to railroad rights-of-way (87 percent within 2 miles, for 46 of the 55 cases where this information was available). Though the typical distance from a railroad track is unknown for suicides by other means, accessibility and availability of a means to complete suicide are significant determining factors in choice of method.
- Fewer decedents had access to firearms than would be expected given national statistics on household firearm ownership. Suicide by firearm is the most common method of suicide in the United States. Although 38 percent of U.S. households have a firearm, a much lower percentage (22%) of individuals in this study had access to a firearm. A lack of easy access to such a widely used method of suicide may

increase the likelihood of an individual turning to an alternative method, such as the railroad right-of-way.

- Choosing a violent method, such as suicide by rail, has been associated with substance abuse or dependence and psychotic disorders (Dumais, Lesage, Lalovic, Séguin, Tousignant, Chawky, & Turecki, 2005). The individuals included in this report were more likely to have a mental disorder (96 percent) or a drinking (62 percent) or substance abuse (58 percent) problem than individuals who chose other suicide methods.

In addition to the aforementioned characteristics, additional information came out of this study which may be useful for the development of countermeasures.

- Incidents tended to occur in urban and suburban areas with relatively high building density. This may help to identify where initial intervention or countermeasure efforts might be focused.
- Incidents did not tend to occur at any particular time of the day. In general, more of the events occurred in the afternoon and early evening than any other time. Although only a few (6) incidents in this report were witnessed, the fact that the incidents often take place during the day indicates that individuals do not typically rely on the cover of darkness to complete the act.
- Fewer than five decedents in this study had a cellular phone in their possession at the time of their death. This may be important for developing countermeasures such as signage which require the individual to call a dedicated help line. However, if the help line number is easy to remember, individuals without a cell phone who visit the site prior to the planned? incident may still be able to call the help line from another telephone.
- Familiarity could be a factor in choice of method. Five decedents had previously attempted suicide by rail. Individuals who attempt to end their lives on the railroad rights-of-way are likely to attempt such an act again.

Limitations. This study offers an assessment of completed suicides on railroad rights-ofway. However, because it lacks a controlled comparison group of non-suicides or suicides by other means, the study cannot offer definitive conclusions about these deaths as differentiated from uncompleted suicides on railroad rights-of-way or suicides by other means. The findings are further limited by the inaccessibility of and lack of cooperation on the part of healthcare workers who were asked but failed to supply medical and mental health records for these decedents. The study also did not include any interviews with train crews or first-responders because access was not provided; investigators relied instead on police reports that summarized those observations.

Psychological autopsy studies rely heavily on interviews with knowledgeable informants. In this study, researchers discarded six cases about which they felt that the quality of the informants' knowledge and observations was either suspect or weak. That said, there remains some degree of variability from case to case in terms of the depth of informants' knowledge, their familiarity with proximal events, the relative recentness of their observations regarding these decedents, and the exact questions that the investigators asked throughout the interview process. A number of decedents in these cases were not involved in a significant relationship at the time of their death; this created some difficulty in locating the best possible informants for the individuals. Having multiple informants for each case would at times lead to conflicting or discrepant observations that had to be resolved, either by further questions to the informants or by the investigator's best judgment in discussion with the research team. In none of the cases studied were the informants noted to be deliberately providing false information. An explanation was sought when there was discrepancy between informants and this resolved the differences in many of the cases.

Another difficulty with the psychological autopsy process is that the next-of-kins' perceptions of how the decedent behaved leading up to the completed suicide may have been clouded by the event. Thus, as a way to justify the outcome, the next-of-kin may offer reasons for why he or she *thought* the individual completed suicide, but those reasons are likely not actual observations about the decedent's behavior leading up to the incident. In light of this, the results of this report deal only with factual information and not with more subjective information.

In a few cases, key informants were unavailable, and others were considered to be insufficiently knowledgeable about the decedent. In addition, the use of multiple investigators increases the potential for variability in interviewing skills, styles, and, therefore, findings. Monthly teleconferences were held for investigators to receive feedback on reports submitted to date. Additionally, a mid-course, follow-up training of investigators was held to attempt to mitigate the variability issue. It should be noted, however, that any changes in interview style and data gathering that resulted from such mid-study training sessions would not be reflected in any earlier cases.

Suicides on railroad rights-of-way are not coded by specific method in national (or international) databases; however, they are included in the overall totals. They are coded as "intentional self-harm by jumping and lying before a moving object" and there is no identification of what that moving object may be (e.g., train, car, bus).

Geographical bias may have been introduced into the sample in at least two ways. Because some States had lengthy procedures for obtaining data and all cases were included without sampling, a State that provided complete data continually and early in the process was likelier to be represented differently from one that provided data just prior to the cut-off for case recruitment. In addition, not all medical examiners complied with the researchers' request for confirmation of the manner of death, citing local or State restrictions that they felt excluded their determination from public information access laws. Thus, a county or State was likely to be underrepresented if investigators could not obtain confirmation that the cases in question had been determined to be suicides and not accidents.

Despite the limitations listed above, this data collection was still able to uncover information that was not previously available in the United States, including the presence of mental disorders and substance abuse among the individuals who complete suicide on the railroad right-of-way. This is the first time that a detailed suicide data collection has been attempted across the United States on railroad rights-of-way. As such, this effort has provided FRA not only with an understanding of some of the defining characteristics of individuals who complete suicide on railroad rights-of-way, but also with information about some of the challenges that arise when collecting detailed information about these events. The lessons learned from this study will be valuable for developing systematic and reliable data collection efforts in the future.

5. Conclusion

Suicides on railroad rights-of-way are relatively rare events, but have lasting impact on witnesses, discoverers, train crews, first responders, and surviving loved ones. Moreover, they cause significant economic consequences for both the railroads (schedule delays, damage to equipment, train crewmember leave, etc.) and society. Identifying potential means to prevent these deaths will be of great benefit to all involved.

This sample of completed suicides on railroad rights-of-way shares much in common with samples of suicides by other means and, in many respects, merely confirms what we already know about those who intentionally take their lives. However, much has been learned through this effort. Notably, the cases studied involved decedents who tended to live near railroad tracks, were less likely to have access to firearms, and were significantly compromised by both severe mental disorder and substance abuse. Additionally, it is important for the development of countermeasure or intervention plans to note that the majority of these suicides occurred in urban or suburban areas (as opposed to rural). They also occurred during both daylight and nighttime hours. A summary of the findings from this effort are included below in Table 3.

Suicidal behavior is the end point on a complex pathway made up of many variables which include long-term vulnerability, an absence of protection, the overwhelming intensity of acute symptoms, and the press of stressful events, all of which ultimately lead to a loss of meaning, purpose, identity, and hope. We believe that the findings from this study may add to our understanding of suicide, and may inform the development of countermeasures that discourage individuals from completing such an act on railroad rights-of-way.

A follow-up document which details potential countermeasures to address suicides is currently being developed by FRA and should be available within the next year. This document will incorporate the information obtained in this report to determine the most effective ways to implement proposed countermeasures in order to maximize their likelihood of success.

Table 3. Summary of Findings

Attribute	Data from Psychological Autopsy of 55 Decedents
Gender	84% male 16% female
Age	33% 30 years old or younger 40% between 31 and 50 years old 27% older than 50 years
Race	96% white 4% nonwhite (IRB restrictions limit the ability to discern quantities smaller than 5)
Sexual Orientation	>90% identified as straight <10% identified as gay, lesbian, bisexual, or transgender

Table 3. (Continued)

Attribute	Data from Psychological Autopsy of 55 Decedents
Marital Status and Offspring	56% single and never married 20% divorced or separated 15% married at the time of death 9% widowed or cohabitating (IRB restrictions limit the ability to discern quantities smaller than 5)
Geographic Distribution	The distribution of the suicides that were studied in this effort was spread across the United States.
Employment Status	43% full- or part-time employment ➢ 19% professional jobs ➢ 27% service industry ➢ 25% laborers ➢ 13% temporary jobs
Government System Involvement	47% involved in nonmedical social system, e.g., welfare or criminal justice system at time of death 15% involved with legal system at time of death
Mental Disorder	96% reported to have had a mental disorder ➢ 47% had been prescribed medications • 40% of these had been reported to have been taking these medications and only half of those were reported to have been effective ➢ 73% reported to have had two or more co-occurring ➢ > mental disorders • 25% of those with co-occurring mental disorders were reported to have been in therapy 64% reported to have had a family member with a mental disorder
Physical Disorder	51% at least one chronic physical illness, including diabetes, chronic pain, cardiovascular disease, endocrine disorders, brain injury, and asthma
Substance Abuse and Toxicology Reports	62% reported to have been heavy consumers of alcohol 58% reported to have been abusing drugs Toxicology Reports (for 43 of the 55 cases) ➢ 51% positive readings • 37% positive for alcohol • 16% positive for illicit drugs

Attribute	Data from Psychological Autopsy of 55 Decedents
	• 16% positive for prescription drugs
Precipitating Factors	94% reported to have experienced at least one stressful and/or adverse event ➢ 35% upcoming negative or humiliating event (court hearing, incarceration, loss of custody) ➢ >15% dissolution of relationship
Past Attempts	44% had attempted suicide at least once in the past ➢ 79% had used at least one low lethality method ➢ 46% had used at least one high lethality method ➢ 9% had attempted on the right-of-way in the past
Witnesses	96% occurred on open track (away from a station) 42% had been observed by community members in the vicinity of the tracks prior to the incident 11% were witnessed directly by bystanders
Time of Day	Most frequent in afternoon and early evenings. However, there was not a clear pattern for when these incidents occur.
Behavior on Tracks	36% were lying on the tracks 27% jumped onto the tracks 27% were wandering along the tracks facing the train
Personal Possessions	Data only available for 29 (52%) or cases ➢ 24% of these cases had no possessions ➢ 31% of these cases had a wallet or purse with ID ➢ 17% had a cell phone (IRB restrictions limit the ability to discern quantities smaller than 5)
Site Accessibility and Significance	49% in high density areas 24% in medium density areas 27% in low density areas 20% in rural areas 55% in suburban residential areas 25% in urban areas
Availability of Firearms	22% reported to have had access to a firearm

ABBREVIATIONS AND ACRONYMS

AAR	Association of American Railroads
AAS	American Association of Suicidology
AIDS	Acquired Immune Deficiency Syndrome
BAC	Blood Alcohol Content
CDC	Center for Disease Control

FRA	Federal Railroad Administration
ME	medical examiner
RRF	Railroad Research Foundation
SOVRN	Suicides and Open Verdicts on the Railway Network
U.S.	United States

REFERENCES

Abbott, R., Young, S., Grant, G., Goward, P., Seager, P., & Pugh, J. Railway suicide: an investigation of individual and organisational consequences. A Report of the SOVRN (Suicides and Open Verdicts on the Railway Network) Project. Doncaster: *Doncaster and South Humber Healthcare* NHS Trust; 2003.

Beautrais, A., Joyce, P. R., & Mulder, R. T. (1997). Precipitating factors and life events in serious suicide attempts among youths aged 13 through 24 years. *Journal of the American Academy of Child & Adolescent Psychiatry.*

Berman, A. L., & Pompili, M. (2011). Medical Conditions Associated with Suicide Risk. Washington, DC: *American Association of Suicidology.*

Botha, J. L., Elmasu, K. A., & Leitzell, P. J. (2010). Suicides on Commuter Rail in California: *Possible Patterns-A Case Study* (No. MTI Report 10-05).

Brent, D. A., Perper, J. A., Moritz, G., Allman, C. J., Roth, C., Schweers, J., & Balach, L. (2007). The validity of diagnoses obtained through the psychological autopsy procedure in adolescent suicide victims: use of family history. *Acta Psychiatrica Scandinavica*, 87(2), 118–122.

Cavanagh, J. T. O., Carson, A., Sharpe, M., & Lawrie, S. M. (2003). Psychological autopsy studies of suicide: a systematic review. *Psychological medicine*, 33(3), 395– 405.

Center for Substance Abuse Treatment. Substance Abuse and Suicide Prevention: Evidence and Implications—A White Paper. DHHS Pub. No. SMA-08-4352. Rockville, MD: *Substance Abuse and Mental Health Services Administration*, 2008.

De Leo, D. & Krysinska, K. (2008). Suicidal behavior by train collision in Queensland, 1990–2004. *Australian and New Zealand Journal of Psychiatry*, 42, 772–779.

Dumais, A., Lesage, A. D., Lalovic, A., Séguin, M., Tousignant, M., Chawky, N., & Turecki, G. (2005). Is violent method of suicide a behavioral marker of lifetime aggression? *American Journal of Psychiatry*, 162(7), 1375–1378.

Eberhardt, M. S., Ingram, D. D., Makuc, D. M., Pamuk, E. R., Freid, V. M., & Harper, S. B. (2001). Health, United States, 2001: urban and rural health chart book. Department of Health and Human Services, Centers for Disease Control and Prevention, National Center for Health Statistics.

Mościcki, E. K. (1997). Identification of suicide risk factors using epidemiologic studies. *Psychiatric Clinics of North America*, 20(3), 499–517.

George, B. (2008). Rail Trespasser Fatalities: Developing Demographic Profiles. Federal Railroad Administration.

Goodwin, R. D., Marusic, A., & Hoven, C. W. (2003). Suicide attempts in the United States: the role of physical illness. *Social science & medicine*, 56(8), 1783–1788.

Haines, J., Williams, C. L., & Lester, D. (2011). The characteristics of those who do and do not leave suicide notes: Is the method of residuals valid? OMEGA--*Journal of Death and Dying*, 63(1), 79–94.

Hepburn, L., Miller, M., Azrael, D., & Hemenway, D. (2007). The U.S. gun stock: results from the 2004 national firearms survey. *Injury Prevention*, 13(1), 15–19.

Kelly, T. M. & Mann, J. J. (1996). Validity of DSM-III-R diagnosis by psychological autopsy: a comparison with clinician ante-mortem diagnosis. *Acta Psychiatric Scandinavica*, 94(5), 337–343.

Kerkhof, A. (2003). Railway suicide: Who is responsible? *Crisis*, 24(2), 47–48.

Ladwig, K.H., Baumert, J.J., 2004. Patterns of suicidal behaviour in a metro subway system: a study of 306 cases injured by the Munich subway, 1980–1999. *Eur. J. Public Health* 14 (3), 291–295.

Lindekilde, K. & Wang, A. G. (1985). Train suicide in the county of Fyn, 1979-1982. *Acta Psychiatrica Scandinavica*, 72(2), 150-154.

Maris, R., Berman, A.L., & Silverman, M.M. (2000). *Comprehensive textbook of suicide*. NY: Guilford Publications.

Mishara, B.L., 1999. Suicide in the Montreal Subway System: characteristics of the victims, antecedents, and implications for prevention. *Can. J. Psychiatr. Rev. Can. Psychiatr.* 44 (7), 690–696.

Phillips, M. R. (2010). Rethinking the role of mental illness in suicide. *American Journal of Psychiatry*, 167(7), 731–733.

Reece, M., Herbenick, D., Fortenberry, J. D., Dodge, B., Sanders, S. A., & Schick, V. (2010). National Survey of Sexual Health and Behavior. Retrieved from http://nationalsexstudy.indiana.edu on November 3, 2011.

Runeson, B., Tidemalm, D., Dahlin, M., Lichtenstein, P., & Långström, N. (2010). Method of attempted suicide as predictor of subsequent successful suicide: national long term cohort study. BMJ: *British Medical Journal*, 341.

Smith, J. C., Mercy, J. A., & Conn, J. M. (1988). Marital status and the risk of suicide. *American Journal of Public Health*, 78(1), 78–80.

Symonds, R. L. (1994). Psychiatric and preventative aspects of rail fatalities. *Social science & medicine*, 38(3), 431–435.

Tanney, B. L. (2000). Psychiatric diagnoses and suicidal acts. *Comprehensive textbook of suicidology*, 311–341.

Timmermans, S. (2005). Suicide determination and the professional authority of medical examiners. *American Sociological Review*, 70(2), 311–333.

U.S. Department of Health and Human Services. (2001). National Strategy for Suicide Prevention: Goals and Objectives for Action. Retrieved from http://sprc.org/library/nssp.pdf.

van Houwelingen, C. A., & Kerkhof, A. J. (2008). Mental healthcare status and psychiatric diagnoses of train suicides. *Journal of affective disorders*, 107(1), 281–284.

van Houwelingen, C. A., Kerkhof, A. J. F. M., & Beersma, D. G. (2010). Train suicides in The Netherlands. CAJ van Houwelingen, Train suicides in The Netherlands. Academisch Proefschrift. Amsterdam: Vrije Universiteit.

Wu, Y., Su, Y., & Chen, C. (2009). Clinical characteristics, precipitating stressors, and correlates of lethality among suicide attempters. *Chang Gung Medical Journal*, 32 (05), 543.

End Notes

[1] In June 2011 FRA began to require railroads to report trespasser fatalities identified as a suicide; however, as of the publication of this document, these numbers are not released publicly.

[2] Currently in FRA review process for publication.

[3] Reporting on Suicide: Recommendations for the Media. Available online at http://www.sprc.org/sites/sprc.org/files/library/sreporting.pdf.

[4] The determination of the manner of death (accident, suicide, homicide, or natural) is made by either a medical examiner or coroner. Medical examiners are licensed physicians, often with training in forensic pathology, who are appointed to their positions. Coroners are elected

officials with no specific medical training; they are responsible for completing death certificates.

[5] While progress through the grief process varies by individual, the principal investigator proposed 6 months as a reasonable time to be sensitive to the informants' grief.

[6] The time period for the suicide by all means comparison group (January 2007– December 2010) is not the same as either the psychological autopsy case group or the all reported rail suicides group (October 2007–September 2010). This is because the CDC estimates for suicides by all means are presented as annual numbers.

[7] The terms "suicide in general" or "suicide by all means" are used in this report to refer to all suicides in the United States, including those on the railroad rights-of-way. Suicides on railroad rights-of-way represent a very small percentage (less than 1 percent) of all suicide cases.

[8] http://www.cdc.gov/injury/wisqars/fatal_injury_reports.html.

[9] American Psychiatric Association (2010). Definition of a Mental Disorder. Retrieved from http://www.dsm5.org/ProposedRevisions/Pages/proposedrevision.aspx?rid=465.

[10] High lethality methods refer to those methods that are generally fatal—e.g., firearms, hanging. Low lethality measures refer to those methods that are less likely to result in death—e.g., cutting the wrist, poisoning with Tylenol.

[11] http://safetydata.fra.dot.gov/officeofsafety/publicsite/summary.aspx.

[12] FRA, Railroad Safety Statistics Annual Report, 1997-2009, Tables 1-2, 10-3.

[13] FRA Accident/Incident Bulletin, 1980-1996, Table 13.

[14] Based on the number of buildings per square mile, block, etc.

[15] Definitions of density used by investigators: low (sparse buildings, lots of space), medium, high (lots of buildings, very little open space).

[16] Definitions of area type used by investigators: rural (open, like fields or woods), suburban (residential), urban (downtown).

[17] In nine cases, the decedent's residence at the time of death was unknown or the decedent was transient, so proximity to residence could not be calculated.

[18] http://www.cdc.gov/injury/wisqars/fatal_injury_reports.html.

In: Mitigating Suicides on Railways
Editor: Frances Diaz

ISBN: 978-1-63484-135-1

Chapter 3

DEMOGRAPHIC PROFILE OF INTENTIONAL FATALITIES ON RAILROAD RIGHTS-OF-WAY IN THE UNITED STATES*

Michael Martino, Scott Gabree and Stephanie Chase

SUMMARY

One of the Federal Railroad Administration's (FRA) primary safety concerns is trespassing on railway rights-of-way. Some trespasser events end as fatalities which can be intentional or unintentional. This project reviews available trespasser data to establish a baseline estimate of intentional trespasser fatalities that occur on railroad rights-of-way and to obtain a basic demographic profile of the individuals involved. This project was especially valuable since at the time of data collection, railroads were not required to report trespasser fatalities and FRA did not collect trespasser incidents on railway rights-of-way that resulted in an intentional death.

Two studies were conducted. Study 1 (June 1, 2006, to May 31, 2007) concluded that 268 trespasser fatality incidents were identified as intentional acts based on a review of railroad trespasser fatality records (RTFRs), state mortality systems, and media reports. During this 1-year time frame, 497 trespasser fatalities were reported by FRA. If no

* This is an edited, reformatted and augmented version of a Research Results paper, RR 13-36, sponsored by the U.S. Department of Transportation, Federal Railroad Administration and issued August 2013.

intentional fatalities are included in this FRA number (reporting guidelines do not require intentional incidents to be reported), then 35 percent of all trespasser fatalities during this time should be considered intentional. Study 2 (June 1, 2007, to May 31, 2010) concluded that 428 trespasser fatalities were determined to be intentional through an active analysis of RTFRs and state mortality systems from the period in question. Those intentional fatalities account for 24 percent of all trespasser fatalities reported during that time frame (1,341 FRA reported fatalities). For Study 2's 3-year period, inconsistencies in data reported by railroads did not permit a precise baseline estimate of intentional trespasser fatality. It can be assumed that those estimates (although not precise) represent the minimum number of intentional deaths that occurred during the studies' time frames, and thus provide an estimate of the overall percentage of railroad right-of-way fatalities.

Results from both studies found that approximately three-quarters of the individuals involved in intentional fatalities were male, which closely mirrored the national gender distribution of suicides by other means. The age of the individuals who completed suicide on railroad rights-of-way tended to be younger than those who completed suicide by other means. No significant patterns were noted for time of day or monthly variation.

Incidents were also examined by State of the participating railroads. The studies showed that Minnesota and Illinois consistently ranked among the States with the highest number of intentional trespass fatalities when adjusted by State population. When adjusted by miles of track within each State, New Jersey, California, and Florida consistently ranked among the highest.

BACKGROUND

Despite significant improvements in many railroad safety related areas, trespasser incidents, both intentional and unintentional, have remained steady. Understanding more about trespasser incidents, including how many of them are intentional acts, may help with the development of more effective mitigation strategies. This effort was the first cooperative attempt by FRA and the U.S. railroad industry to estimate the number of intentional trespasser fatalities occurring on railroad rights-of-way in the United States. Two studies conducted at different time periods provide approximate frequency estimates of the number of intentional trespasser fatalities in the years surveyed.

Objectives

The main objective of this effort was to assess the prevalence of intentional trespasser fatalities on railroad rights-of-way in the United States. Inconsistencies in data reporting throughout the study time frame made it difficult to provide a precise prevalence estimate; however, this study was able to provide estimates of the minimum number of intentional trespass fatalities that occur in a 12-month time period, as well as some basic demographic information about the individuals involved. This effort also provides information about time, month, and location (by State) patterns in the cases identified for the study time frame.

Methods

As noted above, the demographic profiles of suicides on railroad rights-of-way are established through the following two components:

- Study 1: A one-time single year data collection (June 1, 2006, to May 31, 2007)
- Study 2: A continuous 3-year data collection (June 1, 2007, to May 31, 2010)

Study 1 involved a one-time data collection effort during which intentional trespasser fatality data from June 1, 2006, to May 31, 2007, were obtained and reviewed for indication that a trespasser fatality was a suicide that occurred on railroad rights-of-way. The source for this component of the study was data maintained in State mortality surveillance systems, media reports (newspaper articles), and railroad trespasser fatality records (RTFRs).

Study 2 built upon the foundation established in Study 1; however, instead of obtaining all of the data at one time, the investigators actively worked with data sources to acquire data quarterly between June 1, 2007, and May 31, 2010. These data sources included RTFRs and data maintained in State mortality surveillance system. Media reports were not used in Study 2. Some railroads were unable to consistently report during the entire 3-year timeframe of Study 2. Therefore, estimates from Study 2 likely underrepresent the number of intentional fatalities on railroad rights-of-way during those years.

In both studies, duplicate information was often found between sources. In cases where the information between sources was inconsistent, information from FRA/Railroad (e.g., RTFRs) was considered the baseline. State mortality records were then considered followed lastly by media reports (for Study 1 only).

RESULTS

Results from Study 1 and Study 2 are presented separately due to the different data collection strategies employed (see Methods section). Also, note that the data available from each data source varied resulting in different sample sizes for some variables.

Study 1

In Study 1, 268 trespasser fatalities were determined to be intentional. When considering the 497 trespasser fatalities reported by FRA during the same 1-year time frame, intentional fatalities accounted for at least 35 percent of the fatalities on railroad rights-of-way. Information on race/ethnicity was rarely reported in most data sources. Although individual death certificates included this information, retrieving such information was beyond the scope of both studies. For the 268 intentional trespasser fatalities, the following patterns were found in the data:

- A higher proportion of intentional fatalities were male (72 percent). [n = 268]
- Results were analyzed on a State-by-State basis revealing: [n = 268]
    - Top five states for intentional trespasser fatalities after adjusting for population: WI(1), NC, MN, IL, and WA(5)
    - Top five states for intentional trespasser fatalities after adjusting for miles of track: NJ(1), CA, FL, NC, and MA(5)
- Age: Individuals who completed suicide on the railroad right-of-way tended to be younger than individuals who completed suicide by other means (See Table 1). [n = 268]

Table 1. Intentional Fatalities by Age

Age (years)	Study 1	Study 2 (avg.)	Suicides, U.S. - 2009*
<25	20%	19%	13%
25-54	72%	72%	56%
≥55	8%	9%	32%

*Data from the CDC WISQARS database. Percentages are rounded to the nearest whole number.

- Time: The time of day when individuals completed suicide on the railroad right-of-way did not reveal an obvious pattern; however, the most common times were between 6 a.m. and 10 a.m. and between 2 p.m. and 10 p.m. (See Figure 1—blue bars). [n = 152]
- Month: The highest incidence was in June, July, and August; the lowest was in February. [n = 268]

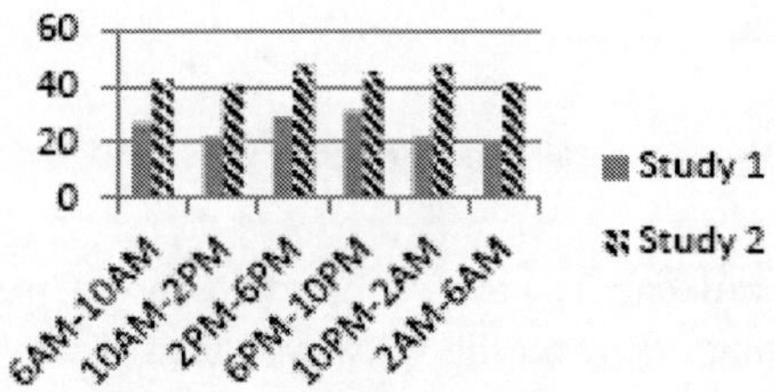

Figure 1. Intentional Fatalities by Time of Day.

Study 2

In Study 2, 428 total intentional trespasser fatalities were identified: 187 in 2007–2008, 157 in 2008–2009, and 84 in 2009–2010. This decline in the number of incidents is more likely due to changes in the number of railroads reporting each year than to an actual decline in the rate of intentional fatalities. FRA trespasser fatality data of this same time frame revealed 488 in 2007–2008, 429 in 2008–2009, and 424 in 2009–2010. A minimum of 24 percent of the trespasser fatalities from this time frame were determined to be intentional. Over this 3-year span, the following patterns were found in the intentional fatality data:

- A higher proportion of intentional fatalities were male (72 percent). [n = 428]
- Results were analyzed on a State-by-State basic revealing: [n = 428]
  - Top five states for intentional trespasser fatalities after adjusting for population: NJ(1), IL, WV, MN, and FL(5)
  - Top five states for intentional trespasser fatalities after adjusting for miles of track: NJ(1), FL, CA, NY, and IL(5)
- Age: The individuals who completed suicide on the railroad right-of-way tended to be younger than individuals who completed suicide by other means (See Table 1). [n = 428]
- Time: The time of day when individuals completed suicide on the railroad right-of-way did not reveal an obvious pattern; however, the most common times were after 2 p.m. but before 2 a.m. (See Figure 1 – striped red bars). [n = 283]

Month: Data for the month-to-month variation could not be analyzed due to inconsistent data collection from month to month.

CONCLUSION

Although U.S. rail carriers are required to report trespasser incidents—including fatalities that occur on the railway rights-of-way—to FRA, as of the time this study was conducted, they were not required to report incidents determined to be suicides. This effort cross-referenced information gathered from States with railroad-supplied trespasser data to identify which trespasser deaths were likely intentional (i.e., suicides). The data allowed us to examine the characteristics of intentional trespasser fatalities on railroad rights-of-way in order to see how they compare, in terms of age, gender, and other pertinent factors such as geographic location and seasonal patterns, with suicides completed by other means. Analyses of this information indicated that approximately three-fourths of intentional trespass fatalities on the railroad rights-of-way involved males; this finding corresponds with national statistics on suicides by other means. The results also showed that individuals involved in intentional trespasser fatalities on the railroad right-of-way tend to be younger than individuals who completed suicide by other means. The data do not allow a precise determination of the prevalence of suicide on the U.S. railroad rights-of-way; however, they do indicate that a minimum of 24 percent (and likely considerably higher than 35 percent) of all trespasser fatalities are intentional acts.

ACKNOWLEDGMENTS

Data collection for this effort was completed by the American Association of Suicidology.

INDEX

D

E

S

T

U

V

W

Y